• LEBANESE MOUNTAIN COOKERY •

LEBANESE MOUNTAIN COOKERY

by

· MARY LAIRD HAMADY ·

with illustrations by Jana Fothergill

DAVID R. GODINE · PUBLISHER · BOSTON

THIS COOKBOOK IS DEDICATED TO
THE SOWERS OF HOPE THROUGHOUT THE WORLD.

First published in 1987 by
DAVID R. GODINE, PUBLISHER, INC.
First paperback edition published in 1995 by
DAVID R. GODINE, PUBLISHER, INC.
Box 9103
Lincoln, Massachusetts 01773

Library of Congress Cataloging in Publication Data

Hamady, Mary Laird, 1948 -
Lebanese mountain cookery.

includes index.
1. Cookery, Lebanese. I.Title.
TX725.L4H36   1987   641.595692   85-45971
Hardcover ISBN 0-87923-618-3
Softcover ISBN 1-56792-020-9

Printed in the United States of America

· TABLE OF CONTENTS ·

· PREFACE ·

SITTI YUMNA HAMADY, Walter's grandmother, was renowned for her cooking expertise all around Baakline, the Lebanese mountain village where she spent a great part of her life. While she lived in the States, her children, in-laws, and grandchildren delighted in her abilities and absorbed her culinary skills, becoming able and exuberant cooks themselves, preserving the tradition of the mountains as well. When I met Walter, he joyfully cooked Lebanese dishes of the most delicious and simple nature, ones he had learned from Sitti Yumna through his mother, Ruth, who had also mastered them to perfection. My culinary background and skills had been somewhat less exotic . . . but then again, what is life if not a challenge?

In 1969 Walter compiled a list of twenty-five recipes using recipe cards from his mother. These became the foundation-block for the book in hand. In 1972 we travelled to Lebanon in order to spend a month researching specific amounts of ingredients and hoping to expand our repertoire of recipes. During our stay we were totally cared for by the extensive Hamady family, and I was able to compile roughly 175 additional recipes.

Then began two solid years of kitchen-testing, which frequently resulted in disaster but eventually produced a refined state of measurements that I felt could become a cookbook. Truth told, the recipes simply stood there and watched as I went full circle, changing them, then changing them back to their original state after I grew up and recognized the perfection in their deceptive simplicity.

Improvisation and cooking "by the hand" or "by the eye," with adjustments by the tongue, are universal methods of cooking, and certainly ones employed by the cooks in the Hamady clan. There is simply no compulsory Lebanese way of measuring and/or cooking. Everyone uses different amounts of spices for the same basic traditional dishes, each spice added according to one's likes, programmed by tastes and observations acquired in childhood. In fact, for some very basic dishes the actual spices used vary from village to village. It goes without saying, that whoever you happen to be talking with on a certain day at a certain time becomes the authority on "how to" make a particular dish. Trying to pin down specifics on method and measurement proved interesting for us all.

Although many years and events in the world have passed since the inception of this book, it is now presented hopefully to all those who believe in preserving and sharing traditions, especially the simple and sacred act of sharing food.

MARY LAIRD HAMADY

· ACKNOWLEDGMENTS ·

THE following people have helped immeasurably with recipes, time, patience, and spirit: Sitti and Jiddi Hamady, Ruth Brackett, Dan and June Hamady, Aunt Celia and cousin Maya Hamady, Aunt Helen and Uncle Adel Musfy and cousin Leila, Aunt Libby and Aunt Alice Hamady, Aunt Jenny and Uncle Sam Hamady. Also many thanks to typist/part-time editor Kate Cruikshank, to Janet Yaeger Burkeland, who helped with the children, to friends Jack and Sondra Beal, Ellen Clark Deeb, Mary Escalante, Mark Lefebvre, to Jana Fothergill for her beautiful drawings, to Sarah Saint-Onge and Sally Rogers for their editing, to Ramzi El Hafez for aid with the Arabic, to my longtime partner and helpmate, Walter Hamady, and to all those others known and unknown who assisted in this endeavor.

MARY LAIRD HAMADY

· LEBANESE MOUNTAIN COOKERY ·

Many of the items below may already be part of your kitchen. If not, they are worth the small investment required because they will make your cooking life much easier. Check local kitchen suppliers, kitchenware areas in department stores, hardware stores, or import shops which specialize in kitchen equipment.

Dairy Thermometer: This may be more difficult to locate than the ordinary deep-fat frying variety, but it is worth the effort if you make yoghurt on a regular basis. These are more finely calibrated, every 2 degrees up to 225° and must *not* be used for fats or sugars whose temperatures will obviously destroy this fine tool. The 2-ounce "floating" dairy thermometer, found through farm supply companies, costs about $10. It is light, beautifully made, and a boon to those who wish to be very accurate when making yoghurt.

Deep-Fat Frying and/or Candy Thermometer: This is manufactured to withstand over 400°. Extremely helpful for any kind of deep- or shallow-fat frying. Essential for syrups, jellies, and jams, and good for making yoghurt if you don't wish to use a dairy thermometer (see above).

Kitchen Scale: Indispensable for accurate measurement. Available in many shapes, sizes, and prices. The wall variety with a fold-out weighing bowl is convenient and compact. Find a scale that will weigh up to 5 or 6 pounds of produce. Those scales which are calibrated to show both American measure and metric are especially good for those of us who are not at ease with the metric system and wish to convert over time.

Kitchen Scissors: Limitless use. Used for cutting fish, chicken, meat, string, for snipping herbs, parsley, noodles, paper, and so on.

MAAMOUL MOLDS : If you go to the trouble of making *maamoul*, the special semolina cookie filled with nuts or dates, you would do well to buy the lovely wooden molds for the cookies. They come in at least four designs, one of which is used exclusively with a date filling. Aside from the cookies, the molds could be used to form the traditional meat-*burghul* mixture — *kibbeh* — or put to use through your own ingenuity.

MORTAR AND PESTLE : The Cuisinart may do it faster and more efficiently, but for those who enjoy working down garlic or walnuts by hand with the simple pounding method, the mortar and pestle are infinitely rewarding. There is something to be said for irregularity of form in, say, crushed walnuts. With the pestle you may miss a part of a nut and smash other nuts to powder; the resulting contrast provides the beauty of both texture and humanness.

OVEN THERMOMETER : After the oven preheats for twenty minutes or whatever the manufacturer recommends, the temperatures on the oven control you set and on the oven thermometer you placed in your oven ought to read the same. I have found they often don't. Buy a good oven thermometer. Many have a metal lip that allows them to stand on a rack. Some also have a hook for hanging over the rungs of the oven rack. Over time and with use, you can determine if your oven bakes too hot, too cool, or just right. Proper control of oven temperature is important.

VEGETABLE REAMER : Essential for hollowing out small cylindrical eggplants and zucchini; good for hollowing out carrots and potatoes as well. Recipes using this tool may be found in the Stuffed Vegetables chapter. Middle Eastern specialty, Oriental, Greek, or Italian stores usually carry this item.

WOODEN SPOONS AND STAINLESS-STEEL WHISKS : Long-handled wooden spoons don't get hot, don't scratch your pans, and are a pleasure to work with. Keep them well oiled. Whisks are indispensable for blending smooth sauces of all varieties and work especially well when incorporating dry ingredients like flour or non-instant dry milk into liquid ingredients.

• SPECIAL PURCHASE ITEMS COMMONLY USED •
IN MIDDLE EASTERN COOKERY

IF you keep a small stock of the items below, you should be able to make any of the recipes in this book.

Most of the ingredients in this list should be available through a Middle Eastern, Greek, or Italian specialty food supplier, if not at your local supermarket.

IN BRIEF
(See below for description of items)

Burghul	Olive oil
Chick peas	Pine nuts
Dried eggplant skins	Pomegranate seeds
Faraykee	Pomegranate syrup
Feta cheese	Semolina
Filo dough	Dried spearmint
Flower waters: rose flower water and	Sumac (ground)
orange flower water	*Tahini*
Kishik	*Zaatar*

Plus (three indispensable items to have on hand):

Yoghurt
Greek olives
Arabic bread

As a matter of course these three essentials are set on the table at most meals. They can and often do become the meal, especially if a simple one is what you have in mind.

BURGHUL : Commonly called "bulgur," referred to as *burghul* throughout this book: partially cooked cracked wheat available in three sizes. Buy some of each. The fine or medium is usually used in the salad *tabbouleh* and the large for dishes in which it replaces rice. See also page 65.

CHICK PEAS: Known in Arabic as *hummous*, roundish yellow beans also referred to as garbanzos. Available dry by the pound or canned. See pages 72–74 for more on cooking and preparing them. Used widely in many dishes. Where they are available fresh and green, chick peas add color and texture to the salad *tabbouleh*.

DRIED EGGPLANT SKINS : Made from small cylindrical eggplants which are hollowed out and the skins dried; stacked about twelve to a package wrapped up in string. After soaking in water these make excellent "casing" for stuffings and provide interesting color and texture. Always buy at least two dozen.

FARAYKEE: Special variety of wheat roasted when it is green, to give it a smoky flavor. This may not be easily available even from Middle Eastern specialty stores. We've included a few recipes for it because it is so interesting. See page 66.

FETA CHEESE: Salty, white, often crumbly cheese, commonly made from sheep milk. Imported varieties from Central Europe are as close to the Old Country variety as any. Sold in bulk or in tins. Used in salads, dips, and certain appetizers. Also eaten plain or covered with olive oil in Arabic bread.

FILO DOUGH : Tissue-paper-thin sheets of pastry dough used for making *baklawa* and other Middle Eastern desserts. Often used to make cheese-filled appetizers. Usually sold in pound or half-pound boxes, fresh or frozen.

FLOWER WATERS: Orange flower water (Arabic: *mazaher*): distilled essence of orange blossoms, used to flavor certain desserts and often added by the drop to Arabic coffee. Rose flower water (Arabic: *maward*): used also to flavor desserts, but not as commonly used as the orange flower water.

KISHIK: Yoghurt, wheat, and milk that are fermented, dried, and ground into a flour-cornmeal-textured substance. Highly nutritious. Tart in flavor, somewhat reminiscent of Romano cheese. Used as thickener in sauces, as porridge, or in endive salad. To make, see page 67.

OLIVE OIL : Buy the very best you can afford: it is essential for good salads. The fruitier, heavier, and darker, the better – that is, the closer to the type used in the Middle East, the better. Some Spanish oils come close. Greek oils, closer. Saica is certainly one of the best. Avoid the brand commonly sold in 8-ounce bottles in the grocery store. Some of the relatives mix a flavorless oil with olive oil when frying foods to give the olive oil flavor without using the wealth of olive oil. The flavor goes far if it's there to begin with.

PINE NUTS : Known in Arabic as *snober*, elongated oval-shaped nutmeat from certain species of pine trees found in Spain and the Middle East. The variety from southwestern United States is wider at one end and has a slightly different flavor. Both varieties are expensive because each nut is encased in a hard thin shell which someone has had to remove. Used in stuffings for meatballs, hollowed-out vegetables, and as garnishes on many different dishes, including decorations of the shortbread cookie *sfoof*.

POMEGRANATE SEEDS : The recipes in this book refer to fresh pomegranate seeds, the red, fleshy, sweet kernels enmeshed in the pomegranate's white web-like casing. Quite an extraordinary fruit. Used in *fattoush* and *baba ghannouj*.

POMEGRANATE SYRUP : Known in Arabic as *dibs rimman*, usually sold in 8- to 12-ounce bottles. Very tart dark concentrate of the pomegranate (not the same as grenadine). The variety known as "molasses" is thicker but could be used in place of the "syrup," only in smaller quantity. Used in *fattoush* salads and *fattee makdoos*.

SEMOLINA : Known in Arabic as *smeed*, ground hearts – endosperm – of hard wheat. Used in desserts such as the rich filled cookie *maamoul* and the cake *nammura*.

DRIED SPEARMINT : Spearmint is usually sold dry, in with herbs or teas. It is used prolifically in Arabic cookery. Never substitute peppermint. In season, fresh spearmint enhances salads, omelets, and fritters; often a bowl of leaves is put out to be eaten in bread with yoghurt and olives. The dried form is used throughout the year in soups, sauces, and salads. If you enjoy Arabic food, you will want to plant your own spearmint patch.

More on growing and drying spearmint : Easy to grow from seed, the plant likes it moist and somewhat shady and spreads like crazy if planted in a good location. It is also easy and practical to dry: Snip stalks before the plant flowers. (If you start early enough in the season, you will get quite an abundant crop of mint before the frost hits or the plants exhaust themselves.) Wash the leaf stalks and shake them dry. Tie them in bunches and hang them upside-down in a well-ventilated, dry, preferably sunless area until leaves become brittle-dry. Then rub or break off leaves and store them in insect-, air-, and moisture-proof containers, again out of the sunlight so they do not discolor. Rub leaves through a sieve to get the crushed form used in cooking.

SUMAC: Sumac berries are arranged in torchlike clumps on large ranging bushes that grow especially well in poor soil. These shrubs cover the mountainsides in the Middle East and are highly regarded for their tart berries, whose tanginess is augmented by the salty sea breeze. The berries are ground into a fine powder which is used in sauces, although it is best known for its role in the savory mixture called *zaatar*.

TAHINI: Sesame seed paste made from cold ground toasted sesame seeds. The variety sold canned or in jars by Middle Eastern specialty stores has a slightly different flavor than that sold in bulk at food cooperatives. Try both. Used in many dips and sauces.

ZAATAR: Arabic for thyme, a special Lebanese mixture of thyme, toasted sesame seeds, and ground sumac. Commonly mixed with olive oil and eaten as paste on Arabic bread; also used in dips, as a topping for *kefta*, and as an appetizer on bread dough. Highly aromatic. Sold by the ounce.

· A FEW NOTES ON OILS AND SHORTENINGS ·

OLIVE oil is used extensively in Lebanese cookery, but the aunts in the Old Country prefer hardened vegetable shortening when an unflavored shortening is called for, specifically for dishes like *menazzaleh* (an eggplant, onion, chick pea, and tomato dish in which the flavors of the individual vegetables should be distinctive, not smothered in olive oil). Already I am in trouble, for my mother-in-law, Ruth, indicates she uses olive oil for this dish. Nevertheless, olive oil adds flavor, which, albeit marvelous, is sometimes uncalled for and undesirable.

Flavorless oil or shortening lends itself well to browning of meat for basic stews. Again the full flavor of the meat is emphasized and doesn't compete with that of olive oil. Personal taste allows all kinds of deviations, but basically olive oil is not used when cooking most meats.

This book employs vegetable oil as a general term for flavorless shortening. Corn and safflower oils work well and are undoubtedly better for you than hydrogenated hardened shortenings. For certain mountain dishes like *makhluta*, a marvelous mixed bean soup, or variations on lentil soup, the lamb-fat-based shortening called *dehen* is critical. A recipe for this follows.

· LEBANESE MOUNTAIN SPICED SHORTENING ·
DEHEN

To my knowledge *dehen* is not readily available at specialty stores. This is a very rural product and is well worth making, even though it may initially appear to be a bother. This recipe makes a very large batch; it will freeze well and may be kept for a very long time.

This is the Lebanese counterpart of American hard shortening – with a difference! *Dehen*, also known as *qawahrma*, is made from the rendered fat of lamb tails, which, on the species raised there, grow to an enormous size. The woolly tail, 9 to 10 inches wide and 1 to 2 feet long, is primarily fatty tissue. When this fat is rendered down and simmered slowly with browned chunks of lamb or coarsely ground lamb and spices, it becomes a natural preservative for the lamb and an economical way to give meaty essence to a dish without actually using much meat. When the *dehen* has finished cooking, it is poured into jars or crocks, which are then sealed with paraffin and stored in a cool dark place.

We have found that lamb kidney fat makes excellent *dehen*. The kidney suet produces *dehen* that is much firmer, though, than the variety made in Lebanon, the texture of which resembles that of lard.

5 pounds lamb suet (*kidney* fat only)
4 pounds lamb
. . .
2 T. plus 2 t. ground allspice
2 T. pepper
4 T. salt
6 T. ground cinnamon

[4 QUARTS *DEHEN*]

Ask your butcher to grind the suet and lamb together coarsely for you. To a large kettle over low heat add the lamb-suet mixture a little at a time until it is all simmering. Skim off any impurities rising to the surface as the fat is clearing. Add spices and stir. The lamb will fry for a long time in the suet, for 5 to 6 hours, before it becomes the proper dark color with dried-up texture. Stir occasionally during cooking period. Fat will clear and meat will settle during this time.

Cool slightly before pouring into crocks, jars, or metal pie tins. Make sure to distribute the meat evenly among the containers. I put it in 4 eight-inch metal pie tins or bread pans and allow it to chill. When cold, tap out the *dehen*, wrap in plastic, and keep in the refrigerator or freezer. Cold storage insures freshness.

• MEATY *DEHEN* •

Aunt Alice makes a meatier *dehen*: 2 parts meat to one part fat, using lamb cut in ½-inch chunks instead of ground. The lamb chunks will shrink and partially disintegrate during cooking.

USE vegetable oil or a hardened shortening, but never butter or margarine. A good heavy pot with a flat bottom and high sides allows the fat to bubble up. Fill pot half full with fat and gradually bring fat to 360° – 375°. Use a cooking thermometer for best results; keep it in hot water until ready to insert in fat, and dry it well before plunging into oil. Avoid heating oil to smoking point, as this indicates fat is breaking down and won't store well; flavor is also impaired.

Be sure food is dry before adding it to hot fat. Drop in only a few pieces at a time and bring fat back to starting temperature. Time the first batch of food to determine length of time for successive fryings.* When pieces are done (golden to darkish brown) remove them with a slotted spoon and drain on absorbent cloth or paper. Skim off any floating particles before adding next batch of food. Remember, the trick is to keep the oil at the same temperature you began with. When you fry fish, let it rest 10 minutes after flouring to dry out a bit. For best results, fry fish and vegetables in separate oil so the flavors don't mix. And of course, fried desserts ought to have separate oil, too. Other than that, experience is your best guide.

When you have finished with the oil, cool it and strain to remove sediment. Store in a tightly covered container in a cool spot.

---

*Nobody in the family *times* deep-fat frying. It's all based on visuals and experience, but it may make you feel more competent and you may have more success the first time around if you use a timer and a thermometer.

· MENU SUGGESTIONS ·

DINNERS

ONCE you get the feel for Middle Eastern foods and acquaint yourself with some of the basic dishes, it becomes easy to put together savory meals for three or for thirteen, emphasizing a variety of textures and flavors as well as colors. Try to include a yoghurt dish, a *tahini* dish, and something with lamb, chick peas, or eggplant if you want to take advantage of the strong roots of Lebanese cookery.

Bread, olives, and a dish of yoghurt or yoghurt cheese are placed routinely on the table, like salt and pepper.

ONE

Baba ghannouj (eggplant and *tahini* dip), page 75
Fatayer bi zaatar (spicy bread pies), page 32

· · ·

Fattee djaaj (chicken, rice, bread, and yoghurt), page 235
Loubieh bzeit (green beans with tomato and onion), page 132
Khyar bi-laban (cucumbers and yoghurt salad), page 116
Bread and olives

· · ·

Amareddeen (pressed apricot paste)
Qahweh (Arabic coffee), page 265

TWO

(very traditional)

Hummous bi tahini (chick pea purée with *tahini*, lemon, and garlic), page 74
Laban and *zeitoon* (yoghurt and olives), pages 44, 51

.   .   .

Fool moudammas (fava beans in oil), page 132

Tabbouleh (tomato, mint, parsley, scallion, and *burghul* salad), page 110

Kibbeh saneeyeh (finely ground meat-*burghul*-onion mixture, with spices, stuffed with pine-nut filling), page 197

.   .   .

Baklawa (paper-thin filo dough with walnuts, cinnamon, and butter, soaked in syrup), page 219

THREE

Tomato, feta, and *zaatar* (a thyme, sumac, and sesame seed mixture), page 79

.   .   .

Samak mishwee or *samak maklee* (baked fish with *taratoor* sauce on the side), pages 175, 176

Sabanekh wa roz (spinach and rice), page 146

Salata-t-hummous (chick pea and parsley salad), page 121

.   .   .

Ghoraybee (ring-shaped butter cookies), page 256

Qahweh, Arabic coffee), page 265

FOUR

Warak areesh bzeit (cold stuffed grapeleaves), page 137

.   .   .

Kefta (ground meat, parsley, onion, and spices), page 202

Taratoor (*tahini* sauce with lemon and garlic), page 59

Menazzaleh (eggplant with chick peas, onion, and tomato), page 111

Laban fattoush II (bread and yoghurt salad), page 120

Saneeyeh-t-battatta (potato pie with meat and pine nuts), page 169

.   .   .

Fruit

FIVE

(to make when it's cold and rainy out and warm in the kitchen)

Fatayer bi flayflee (spicy bread pies), page 30

.   .   .

Sheesh barak (stuffed dumplings with yoghurt sauce), page 95

Salata-t-shamandar (beet salad), page 119

.   .   .

Nammura (semolina cake), page 254

SIX

Avocado with *tahini* dip, page 76

. . .

Sheikh el mahshi (stuffed eggplants in tomato or yoghurt sauce), pages
157, 159
Roz (rice), page 64
Mujaddarah (lentils and rice served with pickled turnips), page 139
Hindbeh bi kishik (endive with *kishik* salad), page 122

. . .

Maamoul (molded semolina cookies filled with nuts or date purée), page
257

SEVEN

*(an all-*maza* buffet, to be expanded indefinitely)*

Kibbeh kras (spiced meat-*burghul* mixture, grilled as patties), page 194
Laban (yoghurt), page 51
Warak areesh bzeit (cold stuffed grapeleaves), page 137
Fatayer bi sabanekh (spinach pies), page 28
Lakhteen bi hummous (pumpkin with *tahini*, chick peas, and onion), page
143
Loubieh bzeit (green beans with tomato and onion), page 132
Fattoush (Aunt Libby's bread salad), page 115
Batinjann bzeit (eggplant with oil and vinegar), page 77

. . .

Sfoof (saffron shortbread), page 255

LUNCHES

Leftovers from dinner; or any one of the soups listed on page 92, accompanied by Arabic bread, a bowl of *laban* (yoghurt), some olives, and fresh
fruit.

ESPECIALLY FOR CHILDREN

Children will eat whatever they are used to eating—and what's put in front
of them—especially if there are no *maamoul* cookies in the cupboard. Below
are some family favorites; those marked with an asterisk (*) mean quick
preparation.

* Eggs and yoghurt with Arabic bread (page 85). Good for breakfast,
lunch, or dinner
* Zucchini fritters with yoghurt on the side (page 110)

Chicken and rice with yoghurt on the side (page 184)
Kibbeh or *kefta* (page 193 or 202). All forms very popular with kids
Chicken *fattee* (page 235)
* Chick pea *fattee* (page 237)
Lentils and rice (page 139)
Potato and chick pea soup (page 103)

ESPECIALLY EXOTIC

Here are some family favorites for adults and children alike. These recipes capture the essence of mountain cookery and are not likely to be found in most Middle Eastern restaurants.

Fattees (pages 235 – 242): Pieces of Arabic bread are toasted in butter, then layered with meat, rice, stuffed eggplants, or chick peas, then covered with a layer of garlic-flavored yoghurt. Pine nuts and parsley decorate the layer of white. Great fun to make and suitable for a group of 6 to 8.

Kibbeh with *kishik* sauce (page 200): A unique sauce, definitely Old Country, in combination with spiced wheat-meat balls stuffed with walnuts and butter.

Kibbeh arnabieh (page 198): The meatballs from above are stuffed with browned pine nuts, then cooked in a *tahini* (sesame paste) sauce.

Sheesh barak (page 95): Little stuffed dumplings, filled with chick peas, parsley, and *dehen*, a spiced fat mixture, are cooked in yoghurt or a sumac sauce. Truly delightful.

Hot tabbouleh (page 101): This treat in the middle of winter consists of *dehen-burghul* wheat, chick peas, and onion, cooked to a thick porridge, then served and eaten with boiled onions and cabbage.

Lakhteen bi hummous (page 143): Fried pumpkin chunks are combined with chick peas, onions, and *tahini* to make a rich and unusual dish.

· I ·

BREADS AND
BREADY APPETIZERS

THE ASPARAGUS SEEDPACKET GRACE

dear lord
let us feel the power
of the life we put into the earth
let us be grateful for the joy
of putting the power of food
and friendship into our bodies
that we may understand
the power of the earth in ourselves.

— *Walter Hamady*

· ABOUT BAKING YEAST ·

Baking yeast comes in three forms: compressed cakes, dry powder in a package, and large granules (sold in bulk by food cooperatives). One compressed cake equals 1 package dry powder equals 1 tablespoon large granules. The powder packages and granules seem to have a longer shelf life than the compressed cakes and take up less room. Store cake and granular yeast refrigerated or frozen in air- and moisture-proof, preferably dark containers. Always check the shelf-life date on yeast before you buy it, and again before you use it.

Yeast organisms are alive and need food, air, and water in order to grow. "Proofing" yeast reactivates the dormant organisms by providing them with these things. It is also a check to make sure the yeast is active before you add it to the dough. To proof, simply dissolve dry or cake yeast in a small amount of warm water; ½ cup is usually sufficient. Yeast organisms multiply quickly given warmth; 110° is considered optimum. Stir in 1 teaspoon sugar to provide the food energy. Let the yeast dissolve, bubble, and foam for 10 minutes. If the mixture does not rise up in the container within that time, assume it is inactive and start again with fresh yeast.

· BREAD SECTION ECONOMICS ·

TO TOAST FRESH ARABIC BREAD

Toasted Arabic bread makes great croutons and is the mainstay of a special salad, *fattoush*, and all the *fattees* (see pages 114-115 and 235-242). For *fattees*, cut one fresh Arabic bread into 6 triangles and separate them to make 12. You will use the triangles for decoration. Break up 2 other breads into bite-sized single-layer pieces. Sprinkle 3 to 4 tablespoons melted butter over all the pieces and bake at 300° for 10 to 15 minutes. Turn pieces every 5 minutes until they are golden brown.

TO TOAST DRIED ARABIC BREAD

When Arabic bread becomes old and stale, dry it out and store in an airtight container. It can be toasted at a later date. When you are ready to use it, break bread in pieces and open them up so they are one layer thick. Place on baking sheet. Sprinkle with melted butter and bake for 10 minutes at 300°. Check occasionally to make sure bread does not get too brown.

TO REVIVE ARABIC BREAD

Arabic bread dries out very quickly, even when stored in plastic in a refrigerator. After 2 or 3 days it may start to crumble. Revive it by sprinkling with a bit of water, or spray it. Then wrap it tightly in foil and heat in oven for 10 minutes at 300°. Once revived, it should be eaten at once, as it will not survive another refreshening.

· ROUND FLAT ARABIC BREAD ·

KHUBUZ ARABEE

Khubuz, pita, Syrian bread, flat bread – the names vary according to the country, but they all refer to the same round flat bread found throughout the Middle East. Lightly browned on top, the bread is 6 to 8 inches in diameter, ¼ to ½ inch thick, and hollow inside. An air pocket forms in the middle during baking, turning the bread into balls of dough skin. They are flattened only after they cool to insure that the two thin sides of bread don't stick together.

Flour, salt, water, and a very little yeast with a dab of oil make up the dough. Although the commercial bread is usually made with an all-white flour, it is not uncommon for mountain bread to consist partially or entirely of whole wheat flour. The rougher flour provides a distinctive chewy texture that is delightful.

Knives, forks, and spoons aren't necessary or much used in a simple Lebanese meal as long as bread is present. A single layer of bread torn into bite-sized pieces serves as "scooper upper" of dips and salads, meat wrapper, olive twister, and plate cleaner. Triangles of bread are often fried in butter, toasted, and used to embellish main courses. They also serve as a bottom layer in *fattees* (dishes using bread as a main component in which meat or chick peas are heaped in layers over the bread, then topped with alternating layers of rice and garlic-flavored yoghurt, over which browned pine nuts, parsley, and crushed spearmint are liberally sprinkled). Dried bread finds its way into salads much as Americans use croutons. And of course, from an untraditional viewpoint, this bread's adaptability to the familiar sandwich is first rate. Meat or cheese, lettuce, tomatoes, and a sprig of cress all gently tucked into the pocket of half a round of Arabic bread not only tastes delicious, but has the advantage of being a compact half-moon that usually doesn't leak or squirt!

In Beirut we saw men on bicycles riding along the highway with long thin poles laden with bread hanging over their shoulders. It wasn't the familiar round bread, for it had the shape of a pocketbook with a handle, making it easy to "ring" onto a stick and carry around. A mixture of spices called *zaatar* (crushed sumac berries with thyme and sesame seeds) filled the insides of these breads. Sumac adds a slightly tart flavor to the highly aromatic and pungent Lebanese thyme. Women who bake bread in the mountains often solve the problem of a simple lunch by blending *zaatar* with olive oil to make a thick paste which they spread over the bread dough as it bakes.

The once prevalent wood-fueled ovens are giving way to gas and electricity, especially in the cities. But the breads still taste the best when baked the old-fashioned way. Mountain or "paper" bread, for which I include a recipe, is a regional specialty made exclusively outdoors.

It is important to knead this dough sufficiently. Proper kneading will insure that the breads puff up, or balloon, during the short, very hot baking time. Otherwise, the air pocket that creates the top and bottom layers of bread may not form completely.

> 1 T. (1 package) dry yeast (see page 20)
> 1 t. sugar
> 1 cup lukewarm water
>   .   .   .
> 15 cups unbleached white flour
> 4½ T. salt
>   .   .   .
> 5 cups lukewarm water (for more nutritious bread,
>   add 1½ cups nonfat dry milk to water and beat well)
> 3 T. olive oil

[25 TO 30 BREADS; FREEZES WELL]

"PROOF" the yeast by dissolving the yeast and sugar in 1 cup lukewarm water for 5 to 10 minutes.

Mix 14 cups flour and salt together in a large bowl, reserving 1 cup flour for kneading. Add 5 cups lukewarm water, oil, and the yeast mixture all at once to flour. Stir with wooden spoon or with hands until dough sticks together. Turn out onto a floured board or cloth and knead very well. Gradually add the reserved flour to keep dough from sticking. Kneading may take 10 to 15 minutes. Dough is ready when it feels elastic; bubbles will break on the surface when you form it into a ball.

Place in a greased bowl and cover with a dry cloth. Let dough rise in a warm place, undisturbed, until it doubles (about 2 hours). Punch dough down. Oil hands and divide dough into 25 to 30 balls the size of small oranges. Again, cover them with a dry cloth and place in a warm spot to rise for 30 minutes.

Roll each ball into a 7 to 8 inch circle, ¼ inch thick or less. Place circles of dough on flat boards or a table. Cover with dry cloth and let rise 1 hour. Meanwhile, preheat oven to 450°.

Place breads on baking sheets, 2 per sheet. When you remove dough rounds to baking sheets, flip them so the top side becomes the bottom side on the sheet. The moister surface is now exposed and rises more easily than the other, which may have dried out slightly. Bake in mid-oven, 2 sheets (4 breads) at a time, for 4 to 6 minutes. After 2 to 3 minutes, the breads will rise and balloon on the baking sheets. Bake 2 to 3 minutes longer, until just slightly brown on the bottom.

Slide breads onto a board to cool, and spray immediately with water. Cover with a damp cloth. When completely cool, flatten them gently with your hand and stack in a pile. Cover stack with a damp tea towel for 2 to 3 hours.

• MOUNTAIN ARABIC BREAD • ("PAPER BREAD")

KHUBUZ MARKOOK

AUGUST 1972

At six o'clock one morning we walked down to Aunt Alice's house to watch her maid Solha making Arabic bread outdoors on a *sājj*, an oven resembling a gigantic Chinese wok with no handles. The *sājj* rested dome-fashion on stones, 5 to 6 inches off the ground. Wastepaper and sticks were shoved underneath it to provide a hot and fast fire.

Solha was preparing the fire when we approached her. At her side lay a large flat-bottomed tin pan. Inside it balls of dough mushroomed, showing off their puffy, smooth satin surfaces. I was getting hungry just looking at them. Late the night before, she had mixed whole wheat flour with water, salt, and a bit of yeast, kneading it all together until it became smooth and very elastic. Six or seven hours of slow rising gave it enough flexibility so it was now ready to be shaped and beaten thin. As we watched her skilled hands pound the dough into a flat perfect circle and then toss it from arm to arm with great ease, we were told she had learned the great art of bread throwing as a child by tossing a washcloth in the air as she watched her mother baking bread.

Sitting cross-legged next to the *sājj*, Solha lit her paper fire and settled down to make the bread. At her feet lay a large flat stone and a round flat-faced pillow which looked like an inflated disk at least 3 feet in diameter. She began by pounding the balls of dough on the stone, one at a time. With both hands she would beat down the outer rim of dough, working quickly inward to the center. The rhythm was steady and strong: one beat, turn the dough, one beat, and turn. Pressure for the pounding came from the heels of her hands. Three well-placed slaps in the center of the dough ended the drumming. Next she threw the bread over her wrist and started tossing it from arm to arm, back and forth. A gentle flip of the fingers sent it over and back onto an outstretched arm. Suddenly the dough ball was transformed into a huge, thin, nearly perfect circle. In some places it was almost transparent. Draping the dough over the waiting pillow, she poked her fire to make sure it was very hot. With one sweep of her hand, she turned the pillow upside down onto the hot *sājj*. Thirty seconds later the bread was bubbly and brown. Quickly she removed the bread to a piece of paper at her side and lifted another doughy puffball to the pounding stone. More drum music! Another pancake of dough underwent transformation.

Soon a tower of aromatic golden disks was all that was left of the dough balls. Solha gave us some bread to taste and watched carefully for our approval. The lovely, speckled brown, exquisitely thin rounds of bread reminded us of the look of handmade paper. Thus the translation of *khubuz markook*: paper bread!

I use unbleached white flour for this bread because we like the smoother texture. If you prefer a healthier bread, mix whole wheat and white flours, half and half.

The big difference between this and the round flat variety lies in the baking. Mountain bread bakes best on a curved surface. A wok makes an acceptable adaptation, if you have no *sājj*.

I find it easiest to mix up the dough at night, say nine o'clock, kneading it for fifteen to twenty minutes. Then cover with cloth and a loose piece of plastic so it doesn't dry out. At five or six (or seven) the next morning, depending on when you wake, you're all set to form the loaves. The bread rises while you rest, and baking can be finished early – before ten a.m.

Mountain bread is served interchangeably with round Arabic bread. Because it is a time-consuming labor of love, it is rare to find and always a treasure when one encounters it.

[25 TO 30 BREADS]

FOLLOW the preceding round Arabic bread recipe exactly, up to the end of the second rising. You now have 25 to 30 balls of dough which have just risen for 30 minutes. Preheat oven to 450°. If you have an electric oven, set it to broil at 450°, placing a baking sheet on the lowest rack. Then turn a

Chinese wok upside down so it rests on the baking sheet. For a gas oven, place an upside-down wok on the floor of the oven.

Combine ¾ cup cornmeal with the same amount of flour. Flatten each ball of dough and dip both sides in the cornmeal mixture. Place them like pancakes in a stack, separating them with wax paper. Make five piles of 6 each (more than 6 may cause the piles to topple over). Cover all the stacks with a cloth so they don't dry out.

Roll out each pancake until it is as thin and round as possible. Then pick up dough and begin to stretch it by flipping it back and forth between your hands. A pizza technique of throwing it up in the air, catching it, and flattening the edges of the circle between your thumb and forefinger works fine. Good luck!

Make a fist with one hand and place dough on top of fist. Then turn dough in circles with other hand, pulling on edges so they get as thin as possible. The shape will be an irregular 14- to 16-inch circle unless you are a wizard at circles.

Drape dough on top of hot wok. Bake 30 to 60 seconds, until lightly browned and bubbly. Peel off and place on baking sheet. Run under broiler for 5 to 10 seconds until dark brown.

Remove to board, spray with water (see Note), and cover with damp cloth. Stack new breads on top of old ones. Cover finished stack with damp tea towels. When bread is pliable (after 2 to 3 hours), fold each in quarters and package in plastic.

NOTE: Traditionally the bread is not dampened at all. Thin spots are crisp and brittle. Finished breads are simply stacked on top of each other. We recommend dampening the bread because we discovered we preferred it pliable, it kept better, and it was also easier to store.

What else is for lunch when you're baking Arabic bread all morning?

• BREAD WITH *FLAYFLEE* OR *ZAATAR* • MIXTURE

FORM an oblong of risen dough ¼ to ½ inch thick and poke it with your fingers to make indentations.

Spread *flayflee* (see page 31) or *zaatar* (see page 8) mixture thinly over dough. Bake at 400° for 10 to 12 minutes.

• BREAD AND *DEHEN* •

MAKE four troughs with your fingers on an oblong of risen dough. Spread meaty *dehen* (see page 10) over the bread. Troughs will corral the *dehen*.

Bake at 400° for 10 to 12 minutes until dough is cooked through. Serve hot.

• BREAD, *DEHEN*, AND EGGS •

MAKE one oblong of risen dough per person and poke several large depressions in it.

Spread lightly with soft *dehen* (see page 9). Make a collar around the edge of each oblong and carefully crack 2 eggs – without disturbing the yolks – into the depressions.

Bake at 350° for 12 to 15 minutes until eggs are set. Salt and pepper to taste.

• BASIC SAVORY PIE DOUGH •

AAJEEN

5 cups flour
1 T. salt

   • • •

2 t. dry yeast (see page 20)
1 t. sugar
¼ cup lukewarm water

   • • •

2 cups lukewarm water (or milk)

   • • •

¼ cup olive oil

[25 FOUR-INCH OR 40 THREE-INCH PIES]

COMBINE flour and salt in large bowl. In another bowl, dissolve yeast and sugar in ¼ cup lukewarm water. Let sit 5 minutes.

Stir yeast mixture into remaining water, or milk, and add to flour mixture. Mix well with wooden spoon and turn onto floured board; knead well for 8 to 10 minutes, until dough is very elastic and smooth.

Place in greased bowl and cover with dry towel. Set dough in warm spot until it has doubled. Punch down and form into a ball. Let dough rest 10 minutes. Divide dough into 25 or 40 pieces. Coat hands with oil and form each piece into a ball. Cover dough balls with dry towel and let rise 30 minutes. Roll balls into circles ¼ inch thick for *fatayer* or fill and form into meat or spinach pies.

• SHORT-CUT PIE DOUGH FOR *FATAYER* •

You may use this dough for *fatayer bi flayflee* or *bi zaatar*, but it does not lend itself well to meat or spinach pies.

4 cups flour
2½ t. salt
6 t. baking powder

. . .

¼ cup shortening

. . .

1½ cups milk

[20 FATAYER]

SIFT together dry ingredients. Rub shortening into mixture with your fingertips until it resembles coarse meal. Add milk all at once and mix with a fork or spoon with light swift strokes, working dough only enough to hold it together.

Knead 30 seconds and roll out onto floured board. Cut into 3- to 4-inch circles, ⅓ inch thick. Spread with *flayflee* or *zaatar* mixture (see pages 31 and 8).

Bake for 10 to 12 minutes at 400°.

• SPINACH PIES •

FATAYER BI SABANEKH

Situ Yumna, Walter's grandmother and renowned cook in the family, considered the pine nuts in this recipe optional, but as an addition they are a visual and flavorful delight.

½ recipe basic savory pie dough (see page 27)

. . .

2 pounds fresh spinach *or* 3 ten-ounce packages frozen spinach

. . .

1 cup finely chopped onion
1½ t. salt
⅛ t. pepper (optional)

. . .

¼ cup lemon juice
¼ cup olive oil

. . .

⅓ cup pine nuts browned in 3 T. butter and drained (optional)
Lemon wedges

[12 TO 15 PIES; FREEZES WELL]

D IVIDE pie dough into 12 to 15 balls and roll into 4-inch circles about ⅛ to ¼ inch thick. Wash, drain, and chop fresh spinach; or cook frozen spinach, drain, and chop. Lightly squeeze out moisture and place in large bowl.

Add onion, salt, and optional pepper to spinach. Mix well and let stand a few minutes. Stir in lemon juice and oil. Add browned pine nuts if desired. It should taste like a good salad.

Place small mound of spinach mixture in center of each round of dough. Form a triangular pie by drawing two sides of dough to the center and pinching shut a seam from the center to the corner. Then draw up the remaining flap of dough and pinch shut the two remaining seams, leaving a small opening to vent the pie in the center. Or make vertical pleats of dough around the filling to form a round open tart. (The former method is more traditional.) Brush with olive oil.

Bake at 375° to 400° for 15 minutes, until brown on top and bottom.

Serve warm or cool with lemon wedges.

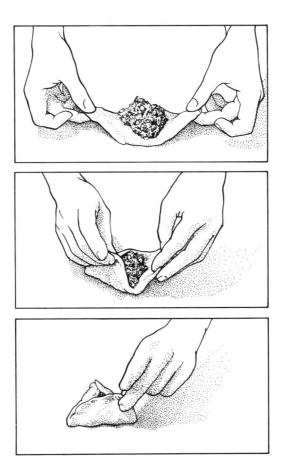

• MEAT PIES •

SFEEHA OR *LAHUM BI AAJEEN*

Both meat and spinach pies are wonderful as a snack or appetizer. They keep well and are sturdy enough to carry around for picnic fare.

½ recipe basic savory pie dough (see page 27)

. . .

1 pound coarsely ground lamb (or beef)
1 cup chopped parsley
1 cup finely chopped onion
1 cup drained yoghurt cheese, or *labnee* (see page 53 and Note)
1½ t. ground cinnamon
1½ t. salt
¼ t. pepper
⅛ t. ground allspice

. . .

½ cup pine nuts, raw or browned in butter (optional)
Lemon wedges

[15 PIES; FREEZES WELL]

D IVIDE pie dough into 15 balls and flatten into 4-inch circles about ⅛ inch thick. Mix all other ingredients together well, adding pine nuts if desired. Put small mound of filling in center of each circle. Form and bake like the preceding spinach pies.

Serve warm or cool, with yoghurt or lemon wedges.

N O T E: Walter's mother, Ruth, says you may use drained cottage cheese or cream cheese. Plain yoghurt is too soupy.

• SPICY BREAD PIES •

FATAYER BI FLAYFLEE

One of the few spicy dishes we encountered, these small Lebanese pizzas are made with *kishik*, a specially treated wheat and yoghurt mixture which is fermented, dried, and then ground into a fairly fine meal. Ruth commented on this recipe, which we acquired from Walter's aunts up in the mountains. Following is an excerpt from her letter, which actually provided another approach to the recipe.

"Sita Yumna [grandmother Hamady] served these *fatayer* with *tabbouleh* at an afternoon lunch party for the ladies. She did not use yoghurt or walnuts. She chopped the onions, added salt and oil, then the paprika, cayenne, and *kishik*; added ½ cup water, then another ½ cup water to wilt the onions. She added sesame seeds last. These can also be made on a flat cookie sheet and cut into squares to serve. The above addition of water would compensate for the onion juice lost because with this second method she used chopped, not grated, onions."

> 1 recipe basic savory pie dough (see page 27) *or*
>> 1 double recipe short-cut pie dough (see page 27)
>
> . . .
>
> FLAYFLEE
>
> 6 T. paprika
> 1 cup olive oil
>
> . . .
>
> 2 cups grated onion
>
> . . .
>
> 1¼ cups *kishik* (see page 67)
> ½ cup sesame seeds
> ½ cup drained yoghurt cheese, or *labnee* (see page 53)
> 6 T. crushed walnuts
> 2 t. salt
> 1½ t. cayenne pepper
> 4 T. lemon juice

[35 TO 40 FATAYER; FREEZES WELL]

PREPARE pie dough and make 35 to 40 circles, 3 to 4 inches in diameter, ¼ inch thick.

Soak paprika in olive oil. Place onions in a bowl, saving the juice. Stir onions and oil together, then add remaining ingredients.

Spread mixture ¼ inch thick on circles of dough. (In the Old Country the women make depressions in the dough with their fingers; these hollows hold the *flayflee* mixture in place and help to prevent the oil from running off.)

Bake on cookie sheets at 400° for 10 to 12 minutes, until the *fatayer* are light brown on the bottom. Stack them on top of each other as you remove them from the oven to keep them moist.

Serve cool. A sprinkle of lemon juice over fresh or aging *fatayer* adds piquancy.

• PIES WITH •
A SUMAC/SESAME-SEED/THYME PASTE

FATAYER BI ZAATAR

One of our favorite ways to greet the morning in the country is to toast a piece of homemade sourdough whole wheat bread, butter it, spread it liberally with *zaatar*, and drizzle olive oil over the top. As I watch the birds at the feeder eagerly cracking into their sunflower seeds, I feel something in common with them: when I smile there are sesame seeds all over my teeth!

Zaatar is a combination of thyme leaves, ground sumac berries, and lightly toasted sesame seeds. The sumac in Lebanon is different from that grown in the States, in large part because it is not "washed" by the rain, as is the domestic sumac. Therefore, it is a lot stronger and more flavorful, with deposits of salt from the air rising off the ocean.

> **½ recipe basic savory pie dough (see page 27) or 1 recipe short-cut pie dough (see page 27)**
>
> **· · ·**
>
> **1⅓ cups *zaatar* (see page 8)**
> **1 cup olive oil**

[15 THREE-INCH PIES; FREEZES WELL]

Roll the pie dough into 3-inch circles, ⅓ inch thick. Make a thick paste of *zaatar* and olive oil and spread thinly on the circles of dough.

Bake at 400° for 10 to 12 minutes. Stack circles in piles as you take them from the oven in order to keep them soft.

• MEAT- OR CHEESE-FILLED PASTRIES •

SAMBOUSEK

Aunt Alice said she usually sent out for the dough to make these delicious appetizer pastries. She also indicated that you could fill them with whatever cheese or meat you had on hand, so use the following as a springboard for whatever bent your creative genius takes!

PASTRY

2 cups flour
1 t. salt

• • •

⅔ cup oil
3 T. cold water

• • •

Oil for deep frying

[40 PASTRIES; FREEZES WELL]

SIFT flour and salt together into a bowl. Beat oil and water in another bowl.

Poke several holes in the flour and pour oil and water into holes. Mix only enough so the dough holds together. Roll out ⅛ inch thick on a floured board and cut into 3-inch rounds. Place 1 tablespoon filling in each center. Moisten the edges of dough with water and fold circles in half. Pleat or crinkle edges.

Deep fry in hot (375°) oil until golden brown. Drain on rack or towel and serve hot.

The following fillings are given in amounts sufficient for 20 pastries each, with the idea that you might like to try more than one filling with each batch of dough.

• I •

8 ounces feta cheese
1 egg, beaten
¼ cup chopped parsley (optional)

Crumble feta into a bowl. Stir in egg; add parsley, if desired.

· II ·

8 ounces bland white cheese (Monterey Jack, Muenster, farmer cheese,
   or ricotta)

· · ·

1 egg, beaten
¼ cup chopped parsley

· · ·

Salt and pepper to taste

If using Monterey Jack or Muenster, melt cheese over very low heat. Stir in
egg and parsley and cook 2 to 3 minutes. Cool. Season to taste.

If using farmer cheese or ricotta, simply mix in the egg and parsley and
season to taste.

· III ·

¼ cup pine nuts
3 T. butter
½ cup chopped onion
8 ounces ground lamb

· · ·

½ t. salt
⅛ t. pepper
½ t. ground cinnamon

· · ·

¼ cup chopped parsley (optional)

Brown pine nuts in butter until evenly light brown. Remove with slotted
spoon. Add onion to butter and fry until medium dark. Add lamb and cook
until it loses its red color.

Then stir in spices and reserved pine nuts; add parsley, if desired.

PICKLED
AND PRESERVED
VEGETABLES

THUMBNAILING THE HILEX

Picking grapeleaves is historical in my family
for generations this is what you stuffed like cabbage
with the multitudes of ingredients, or ate fresh with tabouli.

If you are from the Druse end of the Mediterranean
nobody needs to teach you how to do the harvest,
it is so instinctively implanted on the genetic code
that mere mention of it automatically brings a smile
of greed and glistenings of excitement to the palate.

I was thinking of how dumb it is, or silly, or stupid
but if this enterprise of "let's go pick grapeleaves"
gets suggested among my cousins it is treated on
as explorers planning an atavistic meander to caves.

Grapeleaves do not depend on species to be good,
the ones ripening in the woods are best: shade grown
as big as your hand or bigger, tender & not too thick.
Pick like the best browsing animal would, at random
to not hurt the plants, they'll stay behind in the woods.
You'll need a real good thumbnail on your picking hand
to sever exactly at the hilus, the leaf from the stem,
carefully which you then stack up in your other hand.
We usually take several plastic bags & when they get full
they get transferred to an old Army surplus shoulder bag
so we can be more mobile getting around trees & stuff.
You could take bushel baskets, boxes or whatever
depending on the immensity of your finely honed greed.

The best time to go is right after a rain, early morning
so there will be plenty of birds singing and the insect
population will not have arisen to its Babylonian force!

Many pleasures exist for the picker: the smells of the woods,
the flowers, the leaves themselves – often there are mint patches
crunched by your thoughtless feet, what a great bouquet that is!
Just like being immersed in the tabouli salad you will be eating
with the grapeleaves you are picking! Without doubt, this is heaven!

I love to fling myself on the thick cobwebbing of the vines
sort of like a knocked-out prize-fighter, just hanging there
an astronaut floating in space, thumbnailing juicy specimens
my nose full of early summer, ears full of late spring
eyes & head full of light commanding the last vestiges of dew
exchanging in the air the imprinting of events to memory
as we eat them on a bleak & cold snowbound day.

— Walter Hamady

• PRESERVED GRAPELEAVES •

WARAK AREESH

In the Midwest from the middle of June to early July, there is the greatest abundance of young succulent grapeleaves growing along fencelines and roadsides and meandering through the thickets. Grapeleaves love to mingle with poison ivy. Put on your long pants, heavy gloves, and mosquito lotion, and find the yellow laundry soap.

We used to think that only tender young grapeleaves were suitable for eating, but we have discovered that the darker green, older leaves, after pickling, stand up over time far better than the young leaves. If you plan to use up your grapeleaves during the first year after canning, which, of course, is optimum, young leaves are fine. I suspect the commercial picklers use older leaves, for they are always big and usually tough.

When choosing your grapeleaves, select perfect, unblemished ones and plan to pickle the large dark green ones. *Tabbouleh* salad is often eaten in small tender grapeleaves using the "scooping up" technique. There are all kinds of uses for many forms of grapeleaves. Grapeleaves are often added to jars of dill pickles before canning because they increase crispness, due to their tannic acid.

TO FREEZE

Wash leaves carefully and pat dry with soft towel. Stack according to size in piles of 80 to 100 and wrap in plastic. It's a good idea to put the stacks in a sturdy flat container so they won't break up when you move other items around in your freezer. Freeze immediately.

TO PICKLE

Pickling produces a more leathery-textured grapeleaf, which is even more delicious, to our taste, than frozen leaves.

METHOD I

(The large amount of salt in this method preserves the leaves without additional processing.)

Wash leaves carefully. Place them one at a time in a crock, sprinkling each leaf liberally with canning salt. When the crock is full, invert a plate on top, weight down with a jar full of water, and cover the crock with a towel. Put crock in a cool place for 24 hours, until leaves exude water and become limp.

Take leaves out and arrange them according to size in groups of 20. Roll each group into a tight cylinder and pack into clean wide-mouth quart jars. You may get as many as 10 rolls into each jar. Fill jars to brimming with the brine from the crock. If more solution is needed, boil ½ cup salt with every 4 cups water and cool before pouring over leaves. Or you may prefer to make a hot brine: Bring brine from crock, plus any additional salt-water solution, to a boil, and fill jars to the brim.

Place lids on jars and screw down covers as tightly as possible. The jars may ooze water as time goes on, so check them periodically and top them up with more water so mold won't set in.

We always use Method I, but here's an alternative:

METHOD II

Wash leaves carefully and stack according to size in groups of 20. Roll into tight cylinders and pack firmly into sterilized wide-mouth quart jars.

Add 1 teaspoon salt to each quart and fill to ½ inch from top with boiling water. Put on sterile lid and screw down band securely. Process in boiling water bath for 10 minutes. Cool jars out of draft.

· PICKLED *KOOSA* OR ZUCCHINI ·

KOOSA MAKBOOS

Koosa is the Middle Eastern variety of zucchini squash. It has fuzz all over it, which disappears once the *koosa* is pickled or cooked.

Small *koosa* or zucchini, 4 – 5 inches long, 1½ inches thick

· · ·

Canning salt

WASH squash and remove stem. With a reamer (see page 4), remove seeds and rotate squash to make a shell ¼ inch thick all around. Be careful not to pierce the bottom of the squash.

Sprinkle the squash inside and out with salt. Place them in an enamel or glass container, side by side, and cover with a thin layer of salt. Cover container and keep in refrigerator 2 to 3 days, until squash exude water and are flat and pliable. Drain squash and reserve salt brine.

In a sterile quart jar carefully pack squash vertically. Eight to 10 should fill one jar. Bring reserved salt brine to boil and pour over squash to cover completely. If brine does not fill jar, top up with boiling water, filling jar to overflowing. Cover jars with lids and screw caps firmly tight.

Store in a cool place. Check squash frequently (once a month ought to be fine). Because they are not vacuum-sealed they will ooze water and need to be periodically topped up with sterile water. If they are exposed to air, they will mold.

TO COOK PICKLED SQUASH

Pour off salt brine. Soak squash in fresh water 12 hours, changing water twice. Drain squash.

Fill with basic meat-rice stuffing (see page 153), following those cooking instructions.

Pickling makes the normally mealy-soft texture of squash a tougher one with greater integrity. Nevertheless, be careful not to overcook even pickled *koosa*, or they, like the fresh, will become mushy and unappetizing. Obviously our bias toward the chewy vegetable is showing through here. Ruth had a few comments on the subject: "I soaked the *koosa* two days once by mistake; it tasted like the fresh vegetable. Sitti usually soaked them 12 hours or less and these tended to be too salty and tough." They aren't! Soaking overnight is entirely satisfactory.

• PICKLED TURNIPS •

LIFT MAKBOOS

These pickles are traditionally eaten either with *mujaddarah*, a thick, rich, dark lentil, onion, and rice dish, or with lentil soup and Arabic bread. We like the garlic, but Aunt Libby and Ruth say it's optional.

1 bunch fresh white turnips

· · ·

Salt
1 – 2 raw beets
Large garlic cloves

· · ·

Water or canned beet juice
White vinegar

WASH, destem, and peel turnips and beets. Quarter turnips if small, or cut larger ones into 1-inch chunks. Or slice them if you like that shape better. Pack turnip pieces tightly into sterile jars if you intend to can them, or place in a container to go in the refrigerator.

To each pint container add 1 teaspoon salt, several beet slices, and 1 large clove garlic.

Make a solution of equal parts of water (or beet juice) and vinegar. If you intend to refrigerate the pickles, pour solution as is over turnips. If not, bring solution to boil and fill jars to within ½ inch of top and seal with sterile lids.

Either way, the pickles are ready in a few days, better after a few weeks. They will keep a long time refrigerated.

· SHORT-TERM PICKLED CABBAGE ·

MALFOOF MAKBOOS

---

1 head green cabbage

· · ·

1 raw beet
Garlic cloves
Salt
Cayenne pepper

· · ·

White, red, or white wine vinegar

WASH cabbage. Shred into ¼-inch slices or cut into 1-inch squares. Peel and slice beet. Place several slices of beet, 1 clove garlic, 1 teaspoon salt, and ¼ teaspoon cayenne pepper in the bottom of each quart jar. Pack in cabbage.

Fill jar with vinegar. Cover jar loosely and set in a cool place to ferment for 3 days. Refrigerate to prevent further fermentation.

Serve as part of *maza* (see pages 81 – 82).

· MIXED PICKLED VEGETABLES ·
KHUDRA MAKBOOS

Any one of the following or a combination thereof may be pickled as above. Wash and cut up raw:

broccoli	*koosa* or zucchini
green or wax beans	small onions
carrots	whole button onions
cauliflowers	edible peapods
celery	green peppers
cucumbers	rutabagas
eggplants	turnips

• PICKLED EGGPLANTS •

BATINJANN MAKBOOS

A striking contrast of rich deep red against jet black.

16 whole cylindrical eggplants, 3 – 4 inches long

· · ·

1 cup chopped walnuts
2 cloves garlic, crushed
¼ cup salt
½ cup fresh pomegranate seeds (see page 7)

· · ·

Olive oil and/or vegetable oil

[SERVES 16]

WASH and destem eggplants. Place on a rack in a pan over boiling water. Cover pan and steam eggplants 10 minutes, until they are easily pierced with a fork but not mushy. Cool before stuffing.

Combine nuts with garlic, salt, and pomegranate seeds. Slit one side of eggplants lengthwise and form a pocket by pushing apart the flesh with a spoon. Fill pocket with 1 tablespoon filling and close sides.

Carefully pack eggplants into sterile quart jars. Fill to top with olive oil, or with half and half olive and vegetable oils. Cover jars loosely. Place in cool corner. Fermentation will take place in 7 to 10 days, depending on the weather. Refrigerate after this time to prevent further fermentation.

Serve as a part of *maza* (see pages 81 – 82), and eat in Arabic bread.

• PICKLED EGGPLANTS WITH DRAINED YOGHURT •

Add ½ cup *labnee* (see page 53) to main stuffing recipe. The color is an alarming pink, but the flavor is tart and delicious!

· PICKLED EGGPLANTS WITH GARLIC IN VINEGAR ·

12 cylindrical eggplants, 3 – 4 inches long

· · ·

1 head garlic
¼ cup salt
1 t. cayenne pepper

· · ·

Salt
Red wine vinegar
Water

[SERVES 12]

Prepare steamed eggplants as in main recipe. Cool and slit in 2 or more places.

Separate, peel, and crush cloves of garlic; mix with salt and cayenne. Rub paste into the slits. Place eggplants in quart jars. Add 1 teaspoon salt to each quart. Fill jars to brimming with a solution of 2 parts red wine vinegar to 1 part water. Screw lids on loosely.

Allow eggplants to ferment for 1 to 2 weeks in a cool place. Refrigerate to stop fermentation.

· CURED GREEN OLIVES ·

ZEITOON

Our family has been fortunate to receive wonderful olives from Lebanon once in a while, thanks to relatives; winters are too severe in Wisconsin for olive trees, or we'd have a grove of them. Not to have a recipe for olives in this book when there is so much talk about olives and spearmint and bread would not be right. The first two come from the Old Country, the last from the New.

NOTE: Greek, Italian, or Middle Eastern groceries usually have green olives one may marinate.

· I ·

Green olives, whole or cracked

· · ·

Coarse salt
Water

· · ·

Fresh lemon juice
Olive oil

M AKE a solution of coarse salt and water. (There was no set measure of salt in the mountains because it all depended on the coarseness of the salt. So the women used this old method: add enough salt to water to float an egg.) Bring this brine to a boil and allow to cool.

Pack olives in jars and cover completely with brine. Add 1 to 2 tablespoons lemon juice to preserve color of olives. Seal top of jar with olive oil by floating several tablespoons on top of the brine.

These olives will keep for a year or longer.

· II ·

(This is the best. Thanks to Aunt Libby and Jiddi.)

The lemon trees in Lebanon produce colossal-sized fruit with extremely thick skins. There is a variety called a "bitter lemon" and a tree of the same nature in the orange family. This recipe traditionally calls for a brine made with half lemon and "bitter-orange juice" and half brine, but we have nothing that I know of like this in the States.

Whole green olives

· · ·

Chili peppers (fresh or dry)
Lemons
Thyme leaves (optional)
Orange and lemon leaves (optional)

· · ·

Fresh lemon juice
Salt brine (see preceding recipe)

· · ·

Olive oil

P OUND each olive open to make a crack. Soak in water until olives are no longer bitter, about 2 days. Water should be changed 4 to 5 times in the course of the 2 days. Pack olives into quart jars. To each jar add 2 or 3 chili peppers and 2 or 3 lemon slices. If desired, add thyme leaves. Orange and lemon leaves are often added, too.

Fill jars with a half-and-half solution of lemon juice and salt brine to cover olives. Float several tablespoons olive oil on top of brine to "seal off." Cover and let marinate at least a week.

· III ·

(Thanks to Ruth.)

Green olives, cracked

· · ·

Vinegar
Water
Lemon rind
Thyme leaves

"WHEN I buy cracked green olives, I find them bitter and salty so I pickle them. Drain olives, put in a jar, add half and half vinegar and boiled water, some lemon rind, and a sprinkle of thyme leaves. They are ready to eat in a few days. Love, Ruth."

· PICKLED GREEN PEPPER STRIPS ·

This is a wonderful accompaniment to *baba ghannouj* and *hummous*, but it is definitely not Lebanese. The sweet-sour crunch of this American pickled pepper contrasts with a pungent lemon-garlic eggplant or chick pea dip. We like it so well it has become a tradition at our house to border the *baba* or *hummous* with a green necklace of pepper strips.

Green peppers

· · ·

White vinegar
Sugar

· · ·

Salt

WASH peppers; remove stems and seeds. Cut into strips of uniform length 1 inch shorter than height of jar. Pack snugly in sterile pint jars. Make a solution of 2 parts vinegar to 1 part sugar. Boil for 5 minutes. Add ½ teaspoon salt to each pint jar. Fill with boiling hot vinegar solution to within ½ inch of top. Cover with sterile lids and screw down. Process in boiling water bath for 10 minutes.

• "LEATHER BRITCHES" BEANS •
(DRIED STRING BEANS)

We had no idea when we went to Lebanon that anyone would even know about dried string beans, much less that there would be a recipe calling for them. But *makhluta* (see page 93), a savory mixed bean soup, uses them. Aunt Libby told us she washed and cut up beans and put them in the sun until they dried out. I had found a Native American recipe for doing the same thing a few years before that. One year when we had a colossal crop of beans, the freezer was overflowing and I wasn't up to canning beans. So we dried them instead, using the following method.

THREAD a large needle with strong thread or fishline. Wash and dry green beans and nip off the ends. Run the needle through the center of each bean, crosswise, until you have a string a few feet long. Make a loop of thread and hang beans in a dry, well-ventilated place for 3 to 4 days, until they shrivel up. The beans will droop and look like "little britches"; the texture when cooked becomes leathery. If they are kept out of direct sunlight the color will stay greener.

When they are brittle-dry, store them in an airtight container or plastic. You can sterilize them by placing them in a 250° oven for 15 minutes. Cool before storing.

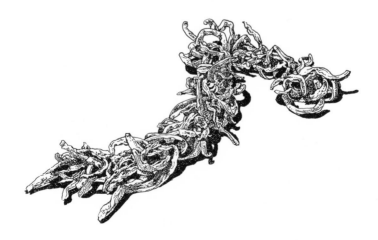

YOGHURT
AND SAUCES

· YOGHURT ·

LABAN

VERSATILE and delicate, creamy tart yoghurt is basic to the Lebanese diet. It is eaten plain in bread with an olive or spearmint leaf and becomes a sauce over meat or stuffed vegetable specialties. Often used as a base for soups or salad dressing, it is also drained and eaten as a thick cream cheese which is especially good when drizzled with olive oil. Recipes which include this nutritious food cover the range from appetizers to desserts, so if you're not already making it yourself, start now. In Lebanon, yoghurt is frequently made from pure goat milk. If you are fortunate enough to be located close to a source of goat milk, treat yourself to some goat yoghurt (*laban anzee*). There is no equal to goat milk yoghurt in terms of flavor, creamy texture, or cooking versatility. The flavor, which has a decidedly distinctive tang, is incomparable, but some may find it an acquired taste. Goat's-milk yoghurt does not need to be stabilized with egg or cornstarch when it is cooked, for it does not separate on heating. It needs only to be reduced by cooking to attain the desired degree of thickness.

Besides being cheaper and better than most commercial yoghurts, the homemade brew is simple to make. The only trick to making it successfully every time is to keep one principle in mind: the bacteria incubate between 90° and 120°. Below 90° they grow slowly, if at all, and much above 120° they are killed. Between 115° and 120° you'll get a good tart yoghurt. Try to keep the milk close to those temperatures during the entire incubation period. You'll also need a good yoghurt culture.

No doubt what my mother-in-law has said is true: "The best cultures come from a household which has a reputation for good yoghurt. Next best is from a commercial yoghurt." Your "starter" is very important. It determines the quality of the finished product. If you can't borrow a starter from a friend, buy a natural form of good commercial yoghurt, with no preservatives, no flavorings. Also available are packages of dried Bulgarian bacteria culture that are more expensive but produce an excellent yoghurt. When the relatives came to the States, they brought over their own yoghurt cultures in handkerchiefs which had been dipped in yoghurt and allowed to dry. The folded-up hankies were simply immersed in warm milk upon arrival.

If you like to putter and have milk and time on hand, try making yoghurt with NO culture. One of Walter's aunts described this method. (Incidentally, we tried it; using cultures is easier and more reliable.)

· YOGHURT FROM SCRATCH ·

Put 1 cup fresh whole, preferably unpasteurized, milk in a bowl. Cover and let sit at room temperature for 2 to 3 days, until it sours and clabbers.

Gather up 2 tablespoons of the more solid "curd" from the clabber and use it as your first "culture." Using the yoghurt-from-culture method, which follows this recipe, make 3 or 4 consecutive batches of yoghurt. To 2 cups milk add 2 tablespoons of the latest batch of yoghurt. Your first batch will be watery, without much flavor.

Save the leftover 30 tablespoons of "attempt" from each of your 3 or 4 tries and use in recipes which call for sour milk. This way nothing really goes to waste. The third time around the yoghurt will start looking and tasting like the real thing. By the fourth, the results should be creamy and tart and thick.

· YOGHURT FROM CULTURE ·

This yoghurt will be thick enough to cut with a spoon. A double boiler is very helpful for yoghurt making. Higher heat may be used without danger of scorching the milk. You can always improvise a double boiler by placing a metal bowl inside a larger pot. You will also need a dairy or cooking thermometer and a quart-size jar.

> **1 quart milk (see Note)**
> **⅓ cup instant dry milk _or_ ¼ cup non-instant nonfat dry milk**
>
> · · ·
>
> **2 T. yoghurt, at room temperature**

Fill clean quart jar with hot water. Cover with tight lid. In a heavy pan or double boiler, heat milk over low fire. Use whisk to blend in dry milk thoroughly. (Adding dry milk will make the finished product really thick.) Heat milk to 180°. Stir occasionally. _Be careful not to scorch it._

Place pan or bowl from double boiler in basin of cold water to speed up the cooling time. Stir until temperature drops to between 115° and 120°. If you have no thermometer, the Old Country method, which is fairly reliable, is to stick in your forefinger. As soon as the milk is cool enough to count slowly to ten, add the culture. Remove pan from cold water and immediately stir in yoghurt. Mix well to dissolve.

Empty hot water from jar and pour in cultured milk. Place wax paper under the cover and screw on tightly. Wrap up jar; keep out of drafts and as warm as possible for 8 to 12 hours. It will be firmly set in 5 hours but more tartness comes with the longer incubation period. Use whatever method works best for you. I turn on our electric oven to the lowest heat for 5 minutes and then turn it off and let it cool down while I am waiting for the milk to heat. Then I line a large pan with a wool cloth, put in the jars, wrap the blanket around to cover, and put a tight lid on the pan. All of this goes in the oven.

If you have a gas oven with a pilot light, wrap up the jars and stick them in; you're all set. Also, Styrofoam coolers make excellent yoghurt makers. Line the cooler with padding; or after placing jars of cultured milk in cooler, pack tightly with towels or a blanket and place lid firmly on cooler. A friend of ours used chicken feathers as padding in her Styrofoam container.

Do not disturb yoghurt during incubation period. If it is jostled at all it may not set up properly. Refrigerate yoghurt after it sets up. Remember to save enough yoghurt from each old batch to start another.

NOTE : Depending on the richness of flavor you want, as well as caloric considerations, use anything from skim milk to coffee cream to make yoghurt. We like whole milk the best but tried using skim milk and found it entirely satisfactory, just not as rich and creamy. If you are fortunate enough to live near a dairy farmer, whole raw milk makes fine yoghurt. Once milk has reached 180°, keep it at that temperature or above for 5 minutes to pasteurize milk. Treat as usual from then on.

• DRAINED YOGHURT CHEESE •

LABNEE

Labnee, drained yoghurt, covered with olive oil is served routinely with any meal in the mountains. Nobody makes their own yoghurt or drained yoghurt cheese in Lebanon because it is so easily purchased. For this recipe you will need an enamel colander and some finely woven cheesecloth or batiste.

1 quart yoghurt (*laban*)

· · ·

Salt

[2 CUPS]

LINE enamel colander with several layers of cheesecloth and pour in yoghurt. Form a bag by gathering up ends and tying a string around the center. Hang for 24 to 36 hours, placing a bowl underneath to catch the whey. (Save the whey and use it in baking recipes calling for water or milk.) The longer it hangs, the firmer it gets.

Lightly salt this creamy cheese before serving. It is remarkably good sprinkled with a few drops of olive oil, eaten in Arabic bread with an olive and fresh spearmint leaf.

• YOGHURT CHEESE BALLS IN OLIVE OIL •

LABNEE BZEIT

---

1 quart *labnee* (see page 53)

• • •

Olive oil

[15 TO 20 YOGHURT CHEESE BALLS]

ROLL *labnee* into balls the size of golf balls. Place in a dish or tray, one layer deep, and refrigerate 24 hours, until they firm up.

Put balls in glass jar and fill with olive oil. Cover jar and refrigerate. Remove jar from refrigerator at least 1 hour before serving to allow oil to thin out.

Spoon oil over balls before serving. Eat in bites of Arabic bread.

• BASIC COOKED YOGHURT SAUCE •

This sauce is good over stuffed or steamed vegetables, or over meat dishes such as *kibbeh* or *kefta*. Traditionally it is also used as a base for cooking the wonderful stuffed dumplings called *sheesh barak* or stuffed meatballs, *kibbeh labneeyee*.

Yoghurt made from cow's milk has to be stabilized with starch or egg white or it will separate during cooking. (Goat's milk yoghurt needs no binder.) Treat this sauce carefully; do not scorch or overheat it, or you will get curdled yoghurt. Old Country "wife-ism" says to stir it in one direction only and to keep the pan uncovered.

> **1 T. cornstarch**
> **1 quart yoghurt**
>
> · · ·
>
> **1 egg or egg white**
>
> · · ·
>
> **1 large clove garlic, crushed (optional)**
> **1 t. salt**
>
> · · ·
>
> **1 T. or more fresh lemon juice (optional)**
> **White pepper to taste (optional)**
>
> [1 QUART SAUCE]

IN a small cup, dissolve cornstarch in 2 tablespoons yoghurt. Whisk this mixture into remaining yoghurt. In a heavy pan or double boiler, begin to heat yoghurt mixture over low heat. Lightly beat 1 whole egg or egg white and gently whisk it into yoghurt. (Egg yolk will color the sauce, so if you want it pure white, just use the white. Leftover yolks will come in handy for other sauces.)

Bring sauce to a simmer, stirring constantly as it thickens up. Cook for 5 to 10 minutes.

If using garlic, crush and add with salt to sauce. For a milder garlic flavor, sauté crushed garlic in butter before adding to yoghurt. Taste for tartness. Add lemon juice and pepper if you think sauce needs them.

Cook sauce for 2 to 3 minutes more. It is now ready to use.

• YOGHURT-*TAHINI* DRESSING •

Excellent over greens and meats, as an alternative to plain yoghurt. Also good as a dip for fresh vegetables. *Tahini* is often added to yoghurt for *fattees*, especially chicken *fattee*.

½ t. salt
1 large clove garlic, crushed
2 cups yoghurt
1 – 2 T. *tahini* (see page 8)
Fresh lemon juice (optional)

[2 CUPS SAUCE]

STIR salt and garlic into yoghurt. Blend *tahini* in well. If not tart enough, add lemon juice to taste.

• WHITE SAUCE •

SALSA-T-HALEEB

Your basic medium-thick béchamel or cream sauce. Good over stuffed egg-plants, zucchini, or baked fish.

4½ T. butter
4½ T. flour
• • •
3 cups milk, scalded
• • •
½ t. salt
White pepper (optional)

[3 CUPS SAUCE]

MELT butter in saucepan over low heat. Quickly whisk in flour, combin-ing well. Do not brown. Still on low heat, allow to bubble for 3 to 5 minutes to get rid of raw flour taste. Flour and butter are slowly cooked to enable flour to expand. If done in less time, the flour will not be able to absorb the liquid properly and its thickening powers will be reduced.

Remove pan from heat and slowly pour in hot milk, stirring or whisking constantly. It will thicken up quickly. Beat well until all lumps are gone and sauce is thin and smooth. Return pan to heat. Stirring frequently, bring to boil over low heat. Cook slowly 5 minutes longer, then add salt, and pepper to taste if desired.

If not using sauce immediately, dot the top with a little butter to prevent a skin from forming.

• GARLIC SAUCE •

SALSA BI TOOM

It's a sure thing this isn't the garlic-potato-lemon-oil sauce served us with grilled chicken in Lebanon, but it's as near as we could come, and it will keep the neighbors away for weeks. (We were told to chew parsley for bad breath. Apparently the chlorophyll does wonders.) When I tried to get amounts more specific than "some potato — you know, it's used as an extender for the garlic," they said, "but I think the ratio is two parts garlic to one part potato." That's not my idea of an extender, considering the individual strengths of the vegetables involved! Rumor said lemon juice, olive oil, and salt were in this mysterious sauce as well; so what you have here is a potato-garlic mayonnaise and it's terrific!

> 1 egg yolk
> ¼ cup fresh lemon juice
> 1 t. salt
> 10 cloves garlic, crushed (see Note)
>   · · ·
> ½ cup olive oil
>   · · ·
> 1 cup mashed potatoes

[1½ CUPS SAUCE]

BEAT yolk, lemon juice, salt, and garlic in a blender for 30 seconds. Turn on blender again and pour olive oil in thin stream until it's all used up. The oil, lemon juice, and yolk will form an emulsion and thicken up.

Gradually add mashed potato and blend until smooth. It will be something like thick heavy mayonnaise.

Serve with grilled chicken or anything else you like garlicky.

NOTE: An English friend, Gillian Riley, suggested this method for preparing garlic cloves. Use a mortar and pestle to remove skin from garlic. Place head of garlic in mortar. With pestle, sharply crack down on point of head to break open cluster. Remove all but number of cloves you want to use. Give each remaining clove a quick sharp hit with pestle to smash it slightly. Skin will come off easily. Cut off any brown ends if you wish, and smash skinned cloves into smooth paste. If you add any salt required for the recipe while making the paste, the grit of the salt will make your job easier.

Other methods include smashing the garlic with the flat of a knife, removing the skin, and then mashing cloves to a pulp; and putting unpeeled garlic cloves into a garlic press, which does a very good job in a hurry.

• LEMON DRESSING •

This dressing enhances hot fried vegetables, hot or cold steamed vegetables (like chard, spinach, cauliflower, or broccoli), or makes a well-known salad dressing for your favorite greens. Also good as a marinade for meats before grilling.

⅓ cup fresh lemon juice
⅓ cup olive oil
⅛ t. freshly ground pepper
½ t. salt
1 clove garlic, crushed

[⅔ CUP DRESSING]

Shake together well.

• *TAHINI* SAUCE •
WITH LEMON AND GARLIC

TARATOOR

Taratoor is the most marvelous sauce – most beloved and versatile. Use it over steamed or fried vegetables – especially cauliflower or fried eggplant. Pour it on fried or steamed fish, *lahum mishwee, kefta, kibbeh,* or just scoop it up in bread with a bit of parsley. It serves as a base for *kibbeh arnabieh* and *lakhteen bi hummous* as well as many other dishes. The richness of the sesame *tahini* combined with the tartness of lemon and the pungency of garlic makes this an unusual and extremely delicious sauce.

> **1 large clove garlic**
> **¾ – 1 t. salt**
>
> · · ·
>
> **½ cup *tahini* (see page 8 and Note)**
>
> · · ·
>
> **½ cup water**
> **½ cup lemon juice, preferably fresh**
>
> [1½ CUPS SAUCE]

MASH garlic and salt into a smooth paste. If you have a mortar and pestle, this is the time to use them. Stir in *tahini*.

Slowly begin to stir in water in small amounts. At first the mixture will get thick – an emulsion of water in oil. Continue adding water. Mixture will become thinner and light tan – an emulsion of oil in water (thank you, Ruth, for the chemistry end of it). Stir in lemon juice and the sauce thickens again. Magic!

NOTE: Half a cup of freshly minced parsley is often added when sauce is used over fried or baked fish. Then, ⅓ cup *tahini* to the above amounts of water and lemon would be sufficient for proper consistency with the parsley.

· IV ·

GRAINS
AND *KISHIK*

love is dust

or lentils and chick-peas

or rocks

or things basic and

inexpensive from the earth.

or love is just everywhere

invisible to laughter and

seen only by those who

have eaten,

by those who can taste and

know a simple recipe.

— *Walter Hamady*

· RICE ·

ROZ

In Lebanese cooking, long-grain rice is usually served with stews, meats, or fish, or just as a side dish sprinkled with browned pine nuts. The short-grain variety is more suitable for meat-rice stuffings and soups, where a splayed-out grain is necessary.

For that "separate grain" texture, so desirable in traditional Lebanese æsthetics, fry the long-grain rice in butter first; the fat coating each grain keeps it separate during the cooking.

The old rule of thumb for rice requires enough water to come an inch over the top of the grain, or up to the first joint on your forefinger. A Japanese friend cooks her rice using this "joint" method, turning out perfect rice every time. She also begins by first washing the rice under cold running water until the water runs clear.

For variety, add 1 teaspoon saffron when you are frying the rice in butter. Saffron rice, lovely in color and flavor, is commonly served, especially with chicken and rice, *roz bi djaaj.*

I. SITTI'S METHOD

(We are told she preferred Uncle Ben's and Arkansas rice.)

1 cup long-grain rice
Boiling water

. . .

2 T. butter
1½ cups water
1 t. salt

[4 SERVINGS]

An hour before serving, place 1 cup rice in bowl. Pour in enough boiling water to cover by 1 inch. Set aside for 20 minutes. Place bowl under cold running water and rinse rice, stirring with fingers until water remains clear in bowl. Drain off water.

Heat butter and add rice. Fry several minutes, until rice becomes transparent. Add water and salt. Bring to boil, reduce heat, cover, and simmer 20 to 25 minutes, until all the moisture is absorbed. Turn off heat. Let rice sit, covered, 5 minutes before serving.

II. (FOR THOSE WHO REBEL AGAINST WASHING RICE)

1 cup long-grain rice
2 T. butter
    · · ·
2 cups water
1 t. salt

[4 SERVINGS]

IN a saucepan, fry rice gently in butter for 5 minutes. Add water and salt. Bring to boil, reduce heat, and cover pan. Simmer 20 to 25 minutes, until water is absorbed. Set pan off heat for 10 minutes before serving.

If you like, sprinkle with 2 tablespoons lightly browned pine nuts. Yoghurt is good on the side.

· *BURGHUL* ·

Burghul (also spelled "bulgar," "burgul," "bulgur") is *parboiled* cracked wheat that usually comes in three sizes: fine, medium, and large. It imparts a nutty flavor and pleasant texture to dishes, especially noted in the salad *tabbouleh*. *Burghul* can be used in place of rice for a "bed" on which to couch stews or stuffed vegetables. For most dishes appearing in this book, the fine or medium is most suitable.

TO WASH AND SOAK *BURGHUL*

(Aunt Libby demonstrated this technique and said if you wash burghul *carefully, it will absorb enough water so it does not have to soak further.)*

MEASURE *burghul* into a large bowl and cover with water. Swirl bowl so the water runs off and carries away any dirt, loose skins, or other debris. Repeat this process several times.

Then cover again with water and gently swirl bowl so a layer of *burghul* flows off; catch it in a strainer. Repeat until all the cracked wheat is washed. The gentle washing action causes any grit present to sink to the bottom of the bowl.

• ROASTED GREEN WHEAT •

FARAYKEE

Totally unknown to us before our journey to Lebanon, *faraykee* was a very special discovery. Wheat is roasted when it is green, giving it a green-brown color. This whole grain has an unusual smoky flavor. Traditionally *faraykee* is served with chicken or tongue, but it is lovely as a simple side dish, used like rice.

1 cup *faraykee* (see page 6)

· · ·

1½ cups water
1 t. salt
¼ t. cinnamon

· · ·

2 T. pine nuts
2 T. butter

[2 TO 2½ CUPS; 3 TO 4 SERVINGS]

QUICKLY wash *faraykee* in a strainer under running water. Drain. Place in saucepan with water, salt, and cinnamon and bring to boil. Reduce heat, cover pan, and simmer 30 minutes. Meanwhile fry pine nuts in butter until evenly golden brown.

When *faraykee* is done, set covered pan off heat for 10 minutes. Fluff with fork. Sprinkle pine nuts over *faraykee* and serve.

• WHOLE WHEAT BERRIES •

While this is not a traditional Lebanese side dish, it is well in keeping with the cuisine. *Hireesee*, a hearty mountain soup, focuses on the whole wheat grain.

These berries, with their marvelous texture and color, are a fine complement to any dish normally served with just rice. (Cook an equal amount of long-grain rice during the last 20 to 25 minutes of the wheat's cooking time and serve them together.) The lovely rich brown of cooked wheat berries set against a pristine white mound of rice pleases many senses. If you serve them side by side in the same bowl, the message is to take some of each.

> 1 t. salt
> 1 quart water
> . . .
> 1 cup whole wheat berries

[4 SERVINGS]

BRING salted water to boil. Add whole wheat berries. Do not stir. Reduce heat and simmer covered for 3 to 4 hours. Check occasionally. Add more water if necessary. When wheat has swelled, some will split.

This is wonderful plain or served with yoghurt.

If you want to cook whole wheat ahead of time, reheat by placing in strainer over gently boiling water and cover until heated through.

• YOGHURT-WHEAT-MILK "FLOUR" •

KISHIK

Kishik, a floury substance with a tart flavor, is one of the mountain cookery staples. It used to be, and maybe still is, made from goat's-milk yoghurt. Whether of cow or goat milk, *kishik* provides excellent nutrition with a very interesting flavor.

By nature a thickening agent, *kishik* is used as a base for *kishik bi dehen*, a porridge (see page 101). Another favorite is *kibbeh bi kishik* (see page 200), stuffed meatballs simmered slowly in a *kishik* sauce. *Kishik* has great potential as a creative ingredient in other sauces and soups. Perhaps the few recipes in this book for its use will inspire experiments in crosscultural cooking. I've even used it as a substitute for grated cheese in salads.

The climate in Lebanon permits making this outside; flat-roofed architecture accommodates the process. I've never tried this recipe due to climate, time, and *kishik*'s availability at a nearby Middle Eastern food store, but Aunt Libby was kind enough to send it, so here it is.

4 cups crushed wheat
3 cups hot milk

. . .

1 T. salt
2 cups yoghurt

. . .

4 cups drained yoghurt cheese, or *labnee* **(see page 53)**
Salt to taste

SOAK crushed wheat in hot milk overnight. Next morning, rub wheat in hands as if you were washing them. Work through bowl carefully. Add salt and yoghurt and let set 24 hours. Add half the drained yoghurt cheese and rub well again. Rub well once more in the evening. Let rest another 24 hours and add the rest of the drained yoghurt cheese. Add salt to taste.

Mix thoroughly twice a day for 3 days. Take out in small portions and place on a sheet to dry. Separate into smaller pieces about every hour or so. Do this until it is dry enough so you can rub it with your hands into a coarse meal. Then sift it and let it dry well before storing.

APPETIZERS AND
DIPS: *MAZA*

M AZA is the Lebanese custom of serving many assorted and delicious hot or cold appetizers with Arabic bread and glasses of a licorice-flavored apéritif called *arak*. There are no limits in terms of variety or quantity of dishes served. It can be as simple as bread, yoghurt, spearmint leaves, and olives, or as elaborate as a seventy-five-dish feast we attended in the mountains which included everything from cheese to frogs' legs. Pickles, dips, cold vegetable dishes, cheese, and several meat, fish, or stuffed vegetable dishes constitute a good *maza*. Accompanied by olives and a dish of yoghurt or yoghurt cheese, some fresh scallions or strips of green pepper and Arabic bread, this "first course" becomes dinner itself!

Coordinate the dishes in the *maza* to include contrast in color, texture, and flavor: something bland with something spicy; something cold with something hot; something crisp with something smooth and creamy. And if you aim to please the visual appetite, you can be sure it makes the act of breaking bread all the more pleasurable.

A typical modest *maza* might include:

> **Hummous (see page 72) (something with *tahini*; very traditional)**
> **Olives (rich, flavorful, and colorful)**
> **Arabic bread (indispensable)**
> **Dish of spearmint leaves (indispensable)**
> **Eggplant and oil (contrast to the *tahini*)**
> **Pickled vegetables (color and texture variables)**

and one of the following:

> **Kibbeh nayee, sfeeha (or *lahum bi aajeen*), sambousek, fatayer**
> **(see pages 194 and 28 − 34) (for richness with meat or pastry)**
> **Drained yoghurt cheese (see page 53) (creamy, tart)**

This *maza* might then be followed by a vegetable or meat entrée, such as chicken *fattee*, and served with *loubieh bzeit* (green beans and tomatoes) and a salad like *tabbouleh* or *fattoush*. Dessert is always your option and often unnecessary.

Maza can be great fun. Its magic lies in its total flexibility. Ruth would entice us to have a "bite" of this or that when we'd make Arabic food together. She'd tear off a bit of Arabic bread and put together a dab of yoghurt and a spearmint leaf plus an olive and give me the "bite" to try. Next she'd slip in a piece of scallion and a spoonful of yoghurt cheese. The first combination happens to be one of our all-time favorites; if you choose Mediterranean olives, you'll have exquisite results.

Hooked by that bite, we tried others. Pretty soon we discovered that if we had Arabic bread in the house, we could convert ordinary leftovers (of any national origin) into a respectable *maza* and clean out the refrigerator as well.

I've often wondered what a Japanese sushi artist would prepare for a *maza!*

• CHICK PEAS •

HUMMOUS

Dried chick peas are economical, taste better than the canned variety, and can be cooked to exactly the degree of softness you like for any particular recipe. They are also simple to prepare, requiring only the forethought to soak them overnight before you intend to cook them. Even this step may be deleted in an emergency.

Although we are addressing chick peas here, the same principles may be applied to any of the dried legumes.

NOTE: The volume ratio of dry to cooked chick peas is 1:3.

TO LONG-SOAK AND COOK WHOLE CHICK PEAS

(This method produces the best color and texture control.)

Wash chick peas well in cold water to remove dust and dirt. Sort through them carefully for any rejects, stones, or other deleterious matter. Drain in sieve. Place them in bowl and cover with four times as much fresh cold water as chick peas. Soak them 8 to 12 hours or overnight. Then discard any that float. Pour chick peas and soaking water into a pan and bring them to a boil. Reduce heat. Skim off any foam and add 1 teaspoon cooking oil. The oil will prevent the pot from boiling over. Cover pan and simmer over low heat for 1¼ hours, until peas are completely tender but not mushy. They should still have integrity. Let the chick peas cool in their own juice. Any leftover liquid can be incorporated into sauces, soups, or broths that require water. You won't lose any of the vitamins this way.

If you need the chick peas softer, for purée purposes, cook them 1¾ hours or use the pressure cooker method below.

TO QUICK-SOAK

(Emergency method to use if you need to split and peel chick peas you forgot to soak.)

Place dried chick peas and four times as much cold water in a pan and bring to boil. Reduce heat, cover, and cook 3 minutes. Set covered pan aside for 1 hour. This accomplishes nearly the same thing as soaking overnight, but it also discolors, or darkens, the chick peas.

You may choose to long-cook them for 1½ to 1¾ hours, adding at least 1 more cup water. Or pressure cook them for 20 minutes using method below, cooling quickly in cold water to reduce pressure.

TO PRESSURE COOK

This is a good method, one we recommend and one that will quarter your cooking time if you remembered to long-soak the chick peas in the first place. The chick peas will be tender yet firm and are suitable for any purpose. Also, there is no discoloration.

Wash and soak chick peas overnight as outlined above. Place 1 inch water in the bottom of your pressure cooker pot. Fit a metal bowl in the cooker, making sure the rim of the bowl is below the top of the pan. Place chick peas and soaking water in bowl and cover pan. Put on weight and bring to pressure over high heat. Reduce heat a bit, and cook under pressure 10 minutes. Then place pressure cooker in sink filled with cold water and bring down pressure quickly.

If you want the chick peas mushy for a purée like *hummous*, cook under pressure for 20 minutes and do *not* place pan in cold water. Let pressure drop of its own accord.

NO-SOAK PRESSURE COOKER METHOD

(The fastest and most reliable emergency method.)

Place washed dry chick peas plus 4 times as much water in bowl in pressure cooker as outlined above. Bring up to pressure and cook 1 hour. Let pressure drop on its own. Texture is not too soft; color is a bit darker than usual. Total cooking time is about 70 minutes.

TO SPLIT AND PEEL CHICK PEAS

Some special recipes, like cold stuffed grapeleaves, *menazzaleh,* and *lakhteen bi hummous,* require skinned and split chick peas. This isn't as painful a task as it might appear. Soak the chick peas overnight as usual (or quick-soak). Drain them, reserving the water to cook them in, and spread them on a tea towel, one layer deep. With a rolling pin gently "rub" the chick peas until they split, but not hard enough to crush them. Pour chick peas and skins into a large bowl and cover with water. Skim off the loose skins as they float to the top, and rub any "resisters" between your hands to loosen up tough skins. Pour off skins and water and return split chick peas to soaking water. Simmer in covered pan for 20 to 30 minutes, until tender.

• CHICK PEA DIP •

HUMMOUS BI TAHINI

This is the dish remembered by all the *faranji* (visitors, implying all those who are not Lebanese), according to my mother-in-law, Ruth. Anyone with any acquaintance with Middle Eastern food knows *hummous*. In fact, a friend of ours who was recuperating from an operation in the hospital begged Walter to make her some *hummous* to speed her recovery.

Scallions, radishes, slices of green pepper (fresh or pickled), even bits of celery, are good served alongside hummous. Parsley and paprika garnishes are basic; and, if you have the taste for it, a bit of cayenne pepper dusted lightly over the top adds an unexpected bang. Use vegetables and Arabic bread to scoop up the dip.

> ⅔ cup dry chick peas (see preceding recipe)
> 2½ cups water
>
> • • •
>
> ⅓ cup *tahini* (see page 8)
> 3 T. chick pea juice
> ⅓ cup fresh lemon juice (or more)
> 1 t. salt
> 1 large clove garlic, crushed (more if desired)
>
> • • •
>
> Parsley, paprika, and olive oil

[2⅓ CUPS DIP; 6 SERVINGS]

RINSE and sort chick peas. Soak overnight in 2½ cups water. Cook in soaking water until very tender, about 1½ hours. You should have 1½ cups. Reserve several tablespoons cooking liquid. Then either mash peas by hand or use blender, reserving a few whole chick peas for decoration.

Stir in *tahini*; then slowly add 3 tablespoons reserved chick pea juice. Continue mixing slowly, adding lemon juice. Mix in salt and garlic to taste.

Everyone likes this a different consistency, so play it by ear. Add more lemon or chick pea juice if necessary.

Pour onto flat serving dish and garnish with parsley and paprika. Decorate with reserved whole chick peas.

Drizzle with olive oil and serve with Arabic bread.

• TOPPING FOR *HUMMOUS* •

Cousin Leila Musfy gave us an enrichment to *hummous*, a variation which makes the *hummous* practically a meal in itself. Pine nuts are browned in butter with finely minced lamb. The combination is sprinkled over the top of a dish of *hummous* in as thick a layer as you care to make. Visitors and friends dipping down into the *hummous* will get a bit of meat, nuts, and the garlic-lemon *hummous* in their bite of Arabic bread.

> ¼ cup pine nuts
> 2 T. butter
> 8 ounces finely minced lamb
> ½ t. salt
> Freshly ground pepper to taste

[1¼ CUPS TOPPING]

OVER low heat fry pine nuts in butter until evenly browned. Remove them and add minced lamb to butter. Brown lamb well for about 10 minutes, and season with salt and pepper. Mix lamb together well with pine nuts and sprinkle in thick layer over one recipe of *hummous bi tahini*.

• EGGPLANT DIP WITH *TAHINI* •

BABA GHANNOUJ

Baba is one of the classic dips, right up there with *hummous* and yoghurt! We like to surround the dish with sweet-sour pickled pepper strips.

1 large eggplant

. . .

1 clove garlic, crushed
1 t. salt
½ cup *tahini* (see page 8)
3 T. water
½ cup fresh lemon juice

. . .

Parsley and/or pomegranate seeds, in season (see page 7)
Olive oil

[3 CUPS DIP; 6 TO 8 SERVINGS]

WASH eggplant and remove stem. Stab in several places with fork. Bake at 400° for 45 to 60 minutes, until pulp is soft and eggplant collapses. In the summertime grill it over charcoal for a special smoky flavor.

Slit and scrape pulp and juices into bowl. You should have about 2 cups. The secret to good *baba* is to scrape all the blackened pulp next to the skin. Add garlic and salt to eggplant. Stir in *tahini* and 3 tablespoons water; slowly stir in lemon juice.

Pour onto flat serving dish and decorate with parsley and/or pomegranate seeds. Drizzle with olive oil and serve with Arabic bread.

• AVOCADO, WINTER SQUASH, •
OR PUMPKIN WITH *TAHINI* DIP

USE 2 cups mashed avocado, winter squash, or pumpkin instead of eggplant in preceding *baba ghannouj* recipe. Be sure the avocado is very ripe and will mash to a smooth paste. If you use squash or pumpkin, steam it until tender and mash to a purée. Neither of these latter two vegetables is traditional, but they show the flexibility of Lebanese cooking — you use what you have on hand and experiment. Develop your own *tahini* variations.

Finely chopped onion and cayenne pepper are good garnishes.

· EGGPLANT ·
WITH WINE VINEGAR AND OIL

BATINJANN BZEIT

To 2 cups eggplant pulp, prepared as for *baba ghannouj*, stir in:

> ⅓ **cup wine vinegar**
> ⅓ **cup olive oil**
> **1 t. salt**
> **1 – 2 cloves garlic, crushed**

[2⅔ CUPS DIP; 6 SERVINGS]

D ECORATE with fresh pomegranate seeds in season (see page 7), parsley, or sweet pickled pepper strips (see page 46).

· BAKED EGGPLANT AND ONION ·
WITH YOGHURT

> **1 large eggplant**
> **1 large onion, unpeeled**
> · · ·
> **1 t. salt**
> **1 large clove garlic, crushed**
> **1½ cups yoghurt (see Note)**
> **Parsley**

[3½ TO 4 CUPS DIP; 6 TO 8 SERVINGS]

W ASH eggplant. Remove stem and sepals. Stab with fork in 3 or 4 places. Place with whole unpeeled onion on baking sheet in 400° oven for 45 to 60 minutes, until eggplant collapses.

Scrape eggplant pulp and juices into bowl. Peel onion and chop into small pieces. Add to eggplant.

Stir in salt, garlic, and yoghurt and pour onto flat serving dish. Garnish with parsley and serve with Arabic bread.

NOTE: You may use half yoghurt and half drained yoghurt cheese (see page 53) for a thicker consistency; or drain yoghurt in a colander lined with a thin cloth for 10 minutes if it is not thick enough to suit your taste.

· DEEP-FRIED EGGPLANT · WITH YOGHURT

BATINJANN KRAS BI LABAN

For variation fry unpeeled *koosa* or zucchini slices.

> 1 large eggplant
> Vegetable oil
> · · ·
> 1 large clove garlic, crushed
> 1½ cups yoghurt
> 1 t. salt
> Parsley

[3½ CUPS DIP; 6 TO 8 SERVINGS]

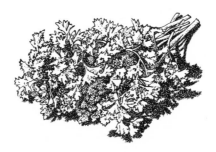

PEEL eggplant and slice in ½-inch thick rounds. Salt them lightly and place in colander to drain for 30 minutes.

In heavy pan, heat 1 to 2 inches of oil to 375°; or test for readiness by frying a sample piece of eggplant. (Oil is ready when eggplant floats, surrounded by bubbles, and browning is apparent. Do not overheat oil to smoking point.) Pat eggplant slices dry and deep fry a few at a time until they are medium-dark to dark brown on both sides. Drain on rack or towels. Mash fried eggplant gently with a spoon to make 2 cups chunky pulp. Add garlic, yoghurt, and salt.

Garnish dip with fresh parsley and eat in Arabic bread.

If there are leftover slices of eggplant, squeeze lemon juice over them, salt lightly, and eat in Arabic bread as bites.

· DIPS WITH *ZAATAR* ·

Zaatar, which means thyme in Arabic, is really a mixture of thyme, sesame seeds, and ground sumac. See page 8 for more about *zaatar*.

I. AN UNUSUAL PUNGENT COMBINATION

1 cup chopped tomato
3 T. olive oil
3 T. *zaatar*
½ cup crumbled feta

[1½ CUPS DIP]

Stir all ingredients together well. Eat in bites of Arabic bread.

II. *ZAATAR* WITH ONION DIP

1 cup onions, slivered in thin crescents (see below)
½ t. salt
3 T. *zaatar*
3 T. olive oil

[1 CUP DIP]

Stir onions and salt together. Mix in *zaatar* and olive oil. Eat with Arabic bread.

(To sliver onion: Peel onion. Slice in half vertically. Place cut half flat and cut onion in ¼-inch slivers, moving in a semicircle, so you have individual pieces.)

III. *ZAATAR* WITH FETA

Simply sprinkle several tablespoons *zaatar* over crumbled feta and serve with bread.

· *KOOSA* OR ZUCCHINI DIP ·

KOOSA BI NAA-NAA

Beleaguered by a gardenful of zucchini, or *koosa* (the Lebanese equivalent)? Or wondering what to do with the pulp from reamed-out summer squash? Make this dip, or try *koosa* fritters.

> 1 cup chopped onions
> 3 – 4 T. olive oil
> 2 cups *koosa* or zucchini pulp, or freshly grated summer squash
>
> · · ·
>
> 1 clove garlic
> ½ t. salt
> 1 t. crushed dried spearmint
> 3 T. water
>
> · · ·
>
> Olive oil
> Lemon wedges

[2½ CUPS DIP; 4 TO 6 SERVINGS]

FRY onions in olive oil until pale yellow. Chop or grate squash pulp and cook with onions for 5 minutes in its own juice, with pan covered. Uncover and cook until juices evaporate, 5 to 10 minutes. Mixture will be soft and light brown. Turn occasionally with spatula.

Crush garlic and stir in salt, spearmint, and water. Sprinkle this sauce over the top of the simmering pulp and cook for a few more minutes. Cool to room temperature and drizzle with olive oil.

Serve with wedges of lemon and Arabic bread.

· VARIATION ·

Use ½ cup more onion. Fry 1 tablespoon chopped green pepper with onion, until both are lightly browned. Slice 4 cloves garlic and add to cooked pulp with onion-pepper mixture. Omit garlic sauce. Simply salt to taste and sprinkle 1 teaspoon spearmint over finished *koosa*. Drizzle with olive oil.

Serve with lemon wedges and Arabic bread.

IDEAS FOR THE *MAZA* TABLE

The dishes are listed under the section of the cookbook where they may be found. Starred items are considered a necessity to any Lebanese meal.

BREADS AND BREADY APPETIZERS

Arabic bread*
Spinach pies
Meat pies
Spicy bread pies
Pies with a sumac/sesame-seed/thyme paste
Meat- or cheese-filled pastries

PICKLED AND PRESERVED VEGETABLES

Green and/or black olives*
Pickled turnips
Pickled vegetables
Pickled stuffed eggplants

YOGHURT AND SAUCES

Yoghurt*
Drained yoghurt cheese
Yoghurt cheese balls in olive oil
Taratoor sauce (*tahini*)

SALADS

Tomato, spearmint, parsley, and *burghul* salad
Bread salad with pomegranate
Cucumber and yoghurt salad
Beet salad
Chick pea and parsley salad
Brain salad

VEGETABLE DISHES

Steamed vegetables with *taratoor* or lemon juice
Deep-fried vegetables with *taratoor* or lemon juice
Artichokes in oil
Egyptian fava beans in oil
Green beans with tomato and onion

Cauliflower fritters
Eggplant with tomato, onion, and chick peas
Cold stuffed grapeleaves
Cold stuffed Swiss chard
Lentils and rice
Pumpkin croquettes
Pumpkin with *tahini*, chick peas, and onion
Spinach and oil
Spinach and rice

FISH AND CHICKEN

Any fish with *taratoor* sauce, served cold
Fish with walnut sauce
Baked fish in tomato sauce

LAMB AND BEEF

Raw or baked *kibbeh*
Broiled *kefta*

MISCELLANEOUS

(The following are more suggestions but are not expanded on by any specific recipe.)

Pistachio nuts, almonds, walnuts
Cold shrimp
Boiled chick peas with a lemon dressing
Dish of freshly picked spearmint leaves*
Fresh raw vegetables
Cold white fish
Raw lamb liver
Caviar
Small pieces of grilled chicken wrapped in "paper bread" (see
        pages 23 – 25)
Arabic sausage and *basterma* (a kind of cured lamb loin with
        spices)
Fried chicken livers
Boiled sliced lamb tongue
Boiled lamb kidneys
Stuffed lamb spleen

EGGS

EGGS AND YOGHURT
Bayd bi laban
85

EGGS WITH RED WINE VINEGAR
86

EGGS WITH POMEGRANATE SYRUP
Bayd bi dibs rimman
86

EGGS WITH SUMAC
86

EGGS BAKED IN *DEHEN*
Bayd bi dehen (qawahrma)
87

CODDLED EGGS IN *DEHEN*
87

EGGS WITH PARSLEY, SCALLION, AND SPEARMINT
Ijjee
87

OMELET WITH PINE NUTS AND PARSLEY
88

BREAKFAST IN LEBANON

Good bread with good cheese is universally accepted as *good* eating. What memorable meals we've made on just that! While traveling in France we would stop to buy a fresh crusty loaf of bread midday, the local cheese specialty, and, of course, a bottle of the local "plonk." When we arrived in Lebanon it was Arabic bread and feta cheese instead of French bread and Camembert.

Basics don't change much from country to country. In Lebanon a most satisfying breakfast consists of a bit of flat bread and some tart, creamy drained yoghurt cheese, or *labnee*, often lightly sprinkled with fruity olive oil and a little salt. Accompany this with a piece of freshly picked fruit or a cucumber and a cup of good strong coffee, and energy starts flowing through early morning veins.

· EGGS AND YOGHURT ·

BAYD BI LABAN

This is one of our all-time favorite breakfasts. Fresh eggs, homemade yoghurt, good olive oil: it's hard to beat, in flavor or nutrition. *Zaatar*, a mix of ground sumac and thyme with sesame seeds, when blended to a paste with olive oil, makes an absolutely perfect spread for plain Arabic bread or whatever toast you enjoy eating the most; and it accompanies eggs and *laban* hand to glove.

Aunt Celia blankets the eggs with yoghurt instead of stirring it in.

> ¼ cup olive oil
> 5 large eggs
> · · ·
> ¼ t. salt
> 1½ cups yoghurt
> · · ·
> Arabic bread
> 3 – 4 cleaned scallions *or* 1 onion

[3 OR 4 SERVINGS]

HEAT olive oil slowly in skillet and add eggs, stirring only *slightly* to break them up. Cook slowly over low heat, shaking occasionally to prevent eggs from sticking to pan.

When eggs are almost set, sprinkle with salt, break them up a bit with a spoon and remove from heat. Stir in yoghurt and serve immediately.

Eat in bites of Arabic bread with either pieces of scallions or a dry onion which has been peeled, quartered, and separated into layers.

• EGGS WITH RED WINE VINEGAR •

PREPARE eggs as in preceding recipe for eggs and yoghurt but omit yoghurt. Stir in ¼ cup red wine vinegar instead. This is unusual, but good. Serve with onion (or scallions) and bread.

• EGGS WITH POMEGRANATE SYRUP •

BAYD BI DIBS RIMMAN

AGAIN, prepare eggs as above but omit yoghurt. Dilute ¼ cup pomegranate syrup (see page 7) with 1 to 2 tablespoons water. Pour over cooked eggs.

• EGGS WITH SUMAC •

PREPARE eggs as above, omitting yoghurt. Mix ground sumac with several tablespoons water and pour over eggs. Serve with scallions.

• EGGS BAKED IN *DEHEN* •

BAYD BI DEHEN (QAWAHRMA)

Another way to serve eggs is bread, *dehen*, and eggs in chapter 1.

½ **cup meaty** *dehen* **(see page 10)**
8 large eggs
Salt and freshly ground pepper

[4 SERVINGS]

P UT 2 tablespoons *dehen* in each of 4 individual baking dishes and place
in 325° oven until *dehen* melts. Break 2 eggs into each dish and bake until
eggs are set, 12 to 15 minutes. Serve immediately with salt, pepper, and
Arabic bread.

• CODDLED EGGS IN *DEHEN* •

M ELT 1 tablespoon *dehen* per egg. Pour *dehen* into bottom of egg coddler.
Carefully break in egg(s) and screw lid firmly on coddler. Immerse
coddler in gently boiling water for 8 to 10 minutes: 8 minutes for a liquid
yolk, 10 for a firmer set.
   A spoonful of yoghurt would be great with these eggs.

• EGGS WITH PARSLEY, SCALLION, • AND SPEARMINT

IJJEE

These are lovely lacy omelet cakes. If you like these, you might like to try
the recipe for *koosa* or zucchini fritters.

3 – 4 T. olive oil
4 large eggs
1 T. flour
¼ cup finely chopped parsley
¼ cup finely chopped scallions
¼ cup crushed dried spearmint, *or* ½ cup fresh chopped leaves
½ t. salt
1 T. water

[ABOUT 15 CAKES; 3 SERVINGS]

IN a skillet, heat olive oil slowly over low heat, until a drop of water will sizzle. Beat together eggs, flour, parsley, scallion, spearmint, salt, and 1 tablespoon water for 30 seconds.

Drop by large tablespoons into oil, keeping them well separated. Fry slowly on one side until golden and flip over to brown the other. Keep finished ones warm in oven until all are done.

Serve with yoghurt on the side.

• OMELET WITH PINE NUTS •
AND PARSLEY

¼ cup pine nuts
3 T. butter

· · ·

6 large eggs
½ t. salt
½ cup finely chopped parsley

· · ·

2 T. butter
Parsley sprigs

[2 GENEROUS OMELETS]

EVENLY brown pine nuts in 3 tablespoons butter until golden. Beat eggs lightly with salt and chopped parsley and stir in pine nuts. Melt 1 tablespoon butter in omelet pan over low heat. When a drop of water will sizzle in pan, pour in half the egg mixture and swirl it around, tilting pan so eggs spread evenly. As the eggs cook slowly, gently lift the sides of the omelet with a fork and let the uncooked portion flow underneath. Continue to cook over low heat until egg is almost set, but slightly soft in center.

Fold in half or roll out onto a warm plate. Keep in 200° oven while making second omelet.

Garnish with sprigs of fresh parsley and serve with Arabic bread.

Yoghurt or yoghurt cheese would be good with this, too, or some feta or string cheese.

SOUPS
AND PORRIDGES

I F you believe in serving food as courses, it's in your best interest to skip this section as a soup course. Label it "main course" and treat it as such. All of these soups, bar none, constitute meals in themselves, quite delightful ones in company with some bread and olives, some yoghurt or cheese, and a salad.

Onion and garlic porridge and mixed bean, rice, and lentil soup are best in the middle of winter, when you need a boost. Try dumplings in sumac or yoghurt sauce for special occasions, when you have some time to play in the kitchen. Lentil, potato, and yoghurt soups are just plain wonderful anytime.

• MIXED BEAN, RICE, AND LENTIL SOUP •

MAKHLUTA

This hearty winter soup recipe is a combination of Ruth's and Libby's versions. Nothing is lost besides an interesting texture if you don't have dried green beans ("leather britches") on hand, so don't let lack of them stop you from trying this. Sitti's version included chick peas, *burghul*, and lentils – no other legumes or rice.

½ cup dry chick peas
¼ cup dry lima beans
¼ cup Egyptian fava beans or small dried beans
¾ cup dried string beans (optional; see page 47)
3 cups water

. . .

10½ cups water, or more
1¼ cups lentils

. . .

2½ cups coarsely chopped onions
⅔ cup *dehen* (see page 9), *or* olive oil, if you must

. . .

¼ cup large *burghul* (see page 6)
¼ cup raw rice
1 T. salt

. . .

½ cup finely chopped onion
1¾ t. ground cumin
¼ t. freshly ground pepper
¼ t. ground allspice
1 t. salt

[3½ TO 4 QUARTS; 12 SERVINGS]

S ORT chick peas and beans and rinse in cold water. Then soak them overnight in 3 cups water. (For short cut, read about cooking beans on page 73.)

After soaking, pour into large pot and add enough water (about 10½ cups) to bring total amount of liquid to 12 cups. Add lentils and bring to boil. Reduce heat, cover, and simmer 45 minutes or until chick peas are tender-firm.

Meanwhile, fry onions in *dehen* until light brown. Add to the soup when beans are tender. Stir in *burghul*, rice, and 1 tablespoon salt; simmer 30 minutes longer. Combine finely chopped onion with spices and 1 teaspoon salt and stir into soup 5 minutes before serving. The porridge should be quite thick with these textures: soft lentil, medium-soft *burghul*, and a tender-firm chick pea.

Serve hot with pickled turnips (see page 41) and Arabic bread.

· DUMPLINGS ·
IN SUMAC OR YOGHURT SAUCE

SHEESH BARAK

Aunt Alice asked us over to her daughter Nadia's house on one of the hottest days in August. Beirut was an absolute oven. Because she knew we were interested in good mountain dishes we'd never tasted, she was working on this incredible soup when we walked in out of the heat. With a smile and her hands full of dough, she kept on making lovely moon-shaped dumplings and told us to make ourselves at home. The kitchen was full of bowls filled with chick peas, yoghurt, brown sauce, chopped parsley, and *dehen*. Fragrant smells assailed us. Alice explained that for lunch we would be having special dumplings stuffed with two different fillings. Even though this was a dish usually eaten in the dead of winter in the mountains when you're starving to death, she'd made both kinds of fillings and both sauces as well so we would have tasted both before we returned to the States. I wish I could say it was only out of politeness that we helped ourselves to seconds of both kinds of dumplings and sauce. For convenience you can make the dumplings ahead of time and freeze them until you need them.

DUMPLINGS

½ recipe basic savory pie dough (see page 27), using ½ teaspoon yeast instead of 1 teaspoon

AFTER the dough has doubled, punch it down and roll it out ⅛ inch thick. Let it rest 10 minutes. Roll it out again to ⅛ inch and cut in 2-inch circles.

Moisten the edge of the circles with water and place 1 heaping teaspoon filling in each center. Fold circles in half. Press edges closed. The doughnut shape is made by pinching the ends of the half-moons together; the alternate shape calls for simply pleating the edges of the half-circle.

If you decide to make both fillings, use one shape for each filling. Leftover dough can be frozen. Filled dumplings also freeze well.

STUFFING I

½ cup meaty *dehen* (see page 10)
⅔ cup finely chopped onion
½ cup crushed or finely chopped walnuts
3 T. finely chopped parsley

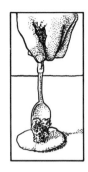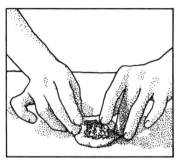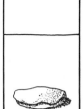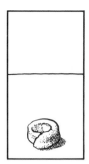

[30 DUMPLINGS; FREEZES WELL]

Heat *dehen* slightly to make it soft enough to combine well with other ingredients.

STUFFING II

This is a basic *kibbeh* stuffing, but Alice's version differs in proportion of ingredients, and since the rest of this is her recipe, here's her *kibbeh* stuffing too.

> **2 T. butter**
> **¼ cup pine nuts**
>
>   · · ·
>
> **8 ounces ground lamb**
> **½ cup chopped onion (optional)**
>
>   · · ·
>
> **½ t. ground cinnamon**
> **⅛ t. freshly ground pepper**
> **½ t. salt**

[30 DUMPLINGS; FREEZES WELL]

Melt butter and lightly brown pine nuts. Remove with slotted spoon. Add lamb to butter and fry until meat loses red color. Add onion and brown lightly. Combine pine nuts with meat and onion. Add cinnamon, pepper, and salt. Let cool before filling dumplings.

Between the yoghurt sauce and the sumac sauce, we found ourselves hard pressed to pick a favorite. I don't think much can beat *laban* (yoghurt) sauce for flavor and texture, but the strangeness and delicacy of the sumac sauce

sauce definitely makes the heartier soup. Sumac sauce takes only stuffing I, but either or both stuffings can be used in dumplings with yoghurt sauce.

SUMAC SAUCE

½ cup dry chick peas

· · ·

⅓ cup *dehen* (see page 9)
1 cup finely chopped onions

· · ·

2 t. salt
2 quarts water

· · ·

¾ cup short-grain rice

· · ·

20 − 22 dumplings filled with stuffing I

· · ·

3 T. ground sumac (see page 8)
3 T. fresh lemon juice
1 cup warm water

· · ·

Crushed dried spearmint leaves (optional)

[6 TO 8 SERVINGS]

Soak chick peas overnight; then skin and split them (see pages 73 − 74). Melt *dehen* and sauté onion to brown lightly. Add chick peas and fry 5 minutes.

Stir in salt and water. Cover and simmer for 20 minutes, or until chick peas are tender. Sprinkle in rice, cover pan, and simmer 20 minutes longer. Drop in dumplings and cook an additional 15 to 20 minutes.

Meanwhile blend sumac with lemon juice and dilute mixture with warm water. Pour sumac sauce into finished soup and heat a few more minutes.

Serve in bowls, and sprinkle with spearmint for an interesting option.

YOGHURT SAUCE

2 quarts basic cooked yoghurt sauce (see page 55),
    made with sautéed garlic
25 − 30 dumplings

· · ·

1 recipe cooked rice (see page 64)

· · ·

Crushed dried spearmint leaves

[6 TO 8 SERVINGS]

To thickened sauce add dumplings; cover and cook over low heat for 15 to 20 minutes, until dumplings are tender.

Be sure dumplings are completely immersed in sauce and kept tightly covered.

Serve over rice and sprinkle with crushed dried spearmint.

• LENTIL SOUP WITH RHUBARB •

SHOURABA-T-ADASS

I thought with something as basic as lentil soup, I wouldn't run into static from the critics; but I couldn't get agreement among Walter, his mother Ruth, and Aunt Libby on onions, spices, *or* method! Here's the scenario, and you be the tongue with discrimination! (W = Walter / R = Ruth / L = Libby).

> **2 pounds meaty lamb bones (neck and leg)**
> **3½ quarts water**
> **1 T. salt**
> · · ·
> **⅓ cup olive oil (W),** *or* **⅓ cup corn oil or fat from meat (R),**
> > *or* **⅓ cup** *dehen* **(see page 9), omitting onions below (L)**
> **2 cups finely chopped onions**
> · · ·
> **1½ cups water**
> · · ·
> **2 cups lentils**
> **¼ cup raw rice**
> **2 − 3 stalks rhubarb (R and W)**
> **Ground allspice, freshly ground pepper, and fresh lemon juice**

[3½ QUARTS; 10 TO 12 SERVINGS]

BRING bones, water, and salt to boil. Skim off froth. Reduce heat, cover, and simmer 3 hours, until meat falls off bones. Strain broth. Pick meat off bones and return meat to broth. You ought to have 3 quarts broth.

Depending on whose option you have chosen, do the following: In a frying pan heat oil and/or fat and brown onions over high heat, stirring constantly so onions don't burn. Fry them 15 to 20 minutes, until they shrivel and turn a very dark even brown (W). They will, in fact, be on the verge of turning black, which does not mean scorched or burned. (R says this is way too dark, to do them medium brown. L says light brown for that method. We like Walter's version because the darkness of the onion is what gives body to the broth flavor.)

Remove pan from heat and stir in ½ cup water; stir vigorously. The water will be absorbed almost immediately and onions will mush up. Add ½ cup more water and return to heat. Simmer until water is almost absorbed and repeat a third time. Onions should be well puréed by now.

Stir in lentils, rice, and 3 quarts broth. Bring soup to boil, reduce heat, cover, and simmer 1 hour, until lentils are quite soft. During last 20 minutes of cooking, add rhubarb, chopped into 1-inch pieces. It should get soft.

Serve hot with sprinklings of allspice, pepper, and lemon juice to taste. (Rhubarb makes the soup tart, but you may still want to add some lemon juice.) Pickled turnips (see page 41) go well with this soup.

• LENTIL SOUP WITH SWISS CHARD •

SHOURABA-T-ADASS BI SILQ

This is Libby's variation of basic lentil soup.

> **1 recipe lentil soup (see page 98), omitting rhubarb and allspice and following directions below**
> **2 – 3 stems Swiss chard**
>
> · · ·
>
> **¼ cup fresh lemon juice**
>
> · · ·
>
> **1 clove garlic, crushed**
> **2 T. olive oil**
> **1 t. ground coriander**

PREPARE the 3 quarts meaty broth. Fry onions until light brown and reserve them for later. Delete the 1½ cups extra water for puréeing onion. Add lentils and rice to salted meaty broth and cook 1 hour, over low heat.

Chop chard stems and add with lightly browned onions to soup 20 minutes before serving. When chard is soft, stir in lemon juice. Meanwhile brown garlic in oil until pale yellow and stir in ground coriander. Blend into soup 5 minutes before serving.

• MEATBALL SOUP •

SHOURABA-T-KAMA

Dowkan, or "Dan," as Walter's father is called, contributed this recipe to the treasury.

1 pound ground lamb or beef
1 cup finely chopped onions
1 cup finely chopped parsley
1 t. ground cinnamon
½ t. ground cumin
¼ t. ground allspice
1 t. salt
⅛ t. freshly ground pepper

· · ·

4 T. butter

· · ·

1 cup chopped onions

· · ·

1 quart lamb or beef broth, meaty if possible
1 t. salt
¼ t. freshly ground pepper
½ t. ground cinnamon
1 quart tomato juice

· · ·

⅓ cup raw rice

· · ·

2 T. chopped parsley

[2½ QUARTS; 6 TO 8 SERVINGS]

To make meatballs, combine meat with onions, parsley, and seasonings. Form into small balls 1 inch or less in diameter. Sauté meatballs in butter until medium brown. Remove and set aside. Add onions to butter and simmer until soft and lightly browned.

In a large pan, mix broth with seasonings and tomato juice. Stir in browned onions and bring to boil. Add rice, reduce heat, cover, and simmer 20 minutes. Drop in meatballs and simmer an additional 20 minutes. Stir in chopped parsley immediately before serving.

· ONION AND GARLIC PORRIDGE ·

KISHIK BI DEHEN

Onions and garlic are the main ingredients in this traditional mountain-peasant breakfast "porridge." You can eat it anytime, and it's actually quite mild and delicious, even though it may not appear so.

> ½ cup *dehen* (see page 9)
> 2 cups onions, slivered in thin crescents
> 6 large cloves garlic, crushed or sliced
>
> · · ·
>
> 1 t. salt
> 1 cup *kishik* (see page 6)
>
> · · ·
>
> 1½ cups water

[2 TO 3 SERVINGS]

MELT *dehen* and sauté onions and garlic until they are light yellow and soft. Stir in salt and *kishik* and turn over several times to blend well. Fry several minutes.

Pour in 1 cup water and stir well. Simmer several minutes and add ½ cup more water. Cover pan and simmer 15 to 20 minutes, until consistency is porridgey. Stir occasionally to prevent sticking.

Eat in bites of Arabic bread.

· *BURGHUL*, CHICK PEAS, AND ONION · PORRIDGE, WITH CABBAGE AND ONION

HOT *TABBOULEH*

Although this dish appears to have nothing to do with the cold summer salad of the same name, the non-seasonal ingredients of wheat, onion, and spices must be the tie that binds. This hearty, strictly mountain dish tastes best in the dead of winter. Ruth improvises a double boiler by placing a large bowl over hot water in a large pan. She said Uncle Kamol was extremely fond of this porridge. You may be, too.

½ cup dry chick peas, soaked overnight (see page 72)

· · ·

2 quarts water
1 t. salt
2 very large Spanish or Bermuda onions, peeled
1 small head cabbage, washed, cored, and quartered

· · ·

½ cup *dehen* (see page 9)
1 cup medium or large *burghul* (see page 6)
2½ cups cooking liquid

· · ·

¾ cup finely chopped onion
1¼ t. ground cinnamon
1 t. ground allspice
2 t. salt
½ t. freshly ground pepper

[4 TO 6 SERVINGS]

SIMMER chick peas in soaking water for 1 hour, until tender; add water if necessary to keep them covered.

Meanwhile, bring 2 quarts water to a boil in a 4- to 6-quart pot. Add 1 teaspoon salt and onions. You will be gently simmering them for 30 to 60 minutes, depending on their size. Thirty minutes ought to find the jumbo onions half done. At that time add cabbage and simmer another 25 to 30 minutes, until both onions and cabbage are very tender. Keep cabbage and onions warm until porridge is done by placing on rack (or steamer) over hot cooking liquid.

Melt *dehen* in double boiler. Stir in *burghul* and mix thoroughly. Drain chick peas, reserving the juice. Add chick peas to *burghul*. Cover pan and steam 20 minutes.

Add enough cabbage-onion cooking liquid to chick pea juice to equal 1½ cups. Stir into *burghul* mixture. Steam 20 more minutes. Add another cup cabbage-onion liquid and cook another 20 minutes. When the liquid has all been absorbed, mix chopped onion with cinnamon, allspice, 2 teaspoons salt, and pepper. Stir into *burghul* and steam a final 20 minutes.

To serve, place cabbage and quartered onions on a platter and dish up the porridge in a separate serving bowl. Everyone scoops up bites of porridge in large pieces of cabbage and onion.

• POTATO SOUP •

SHOURABA-T-BATTATTA

Dehen, spearmint, and lemon are unusual additions to this version of the familiar potato soup. Especially good during long, snowy winters or the cold spells of late fall.

> ⅔ **cup dry chick peas, soaked overnight (see page 72)**
>
> · · ·
>
> ½ **cup** *dehen* **(see page 9)**
> **1 cup chopped onions**
>
> · · ·
>
> **Water**
>
> · · ·
>
> ½ **cup raw short-grain rice**
> **2 t. salt**
> 1⅓ **pounds potatoes, peeled and cut in ¾-inch chunks (4 cups)**
>
> · · ·
>
> **Fresh lemon juice**
> **Crushed dried spearmint**

[2½ QUARTS; 6 TO 8 SERVINGS]

COOK soaked chick peas until tender, 1¼ hours. Drain, reserving cooking water. Melt *dehen* in a 3-quart pan and sauté onions until limp, transparent, and brown around the edges.

Measure reserved cooking water. Add water to equal 5½ cups liquid. Add with chick peas to *dehen* and onion mixture. Stir in rice, salt, and potatoes. Bring quickly to boil, reduce heat, cover, and simmer 20 to 25 minutes, until potatoes and rice are tender. Thin with water if too thick for your taste.

Serve hot, adding 1 tablespoon lemon juice and ¼ to ½ teaspoon spearmint to each serving.

· YOGHURT SOUP ·

LABNEEYEE

Certainly one of our all-time favorites. Use the larger amount of water when making the broth if you prefer soup to porridge. Stuffed *kibbeh* balls can be added to this soup to make it a satisfying one-dish meal, *kibbeh labneeyee*.

One of Walter's aunts told us to stir in only one direction when cooking any kind of yoghurt sauce, "because that's the way it should be done."

1 pound or more meaty lamb bones
2 – 3 T. vegetable oil

· · ·

2½ – 3½ cups water
1 large stick cinnamon
1 t. salt

· · ·

½ t. ground cinnamon
½ t. salt
⅛ – ¼ t. white pepper
½ cup raw short-grain rice

· · ·

1 quart yoghurt
1 T. cornstarch dissolved in 2 T. water

· · ·

Crushed dried spearmint

[1½ TO 2 QUARTS; 6 SERVINGS]

BROWN bones well in hot oil. Add water, cinnamon stick, and 1 teaspoon salt. Bring to a boil and remove any scum. Reduce heat, cover pan, and simmer 2 to 3 hours, until meat falls from bones. Remove bones and pick them clean. Strain broth and return with meat to pan.

Add ground cinnamon, ½ teaspoon salt, and white pepper. (White variety doesn't speckle the white sauce.) Bring to low boil. Sprinkle rice into soup. Reduce heat, cover pan, and cook 20 minutes.

Blend yoghurt with cornstarch mixture. When rice is tender, pour yoghurt into soup and stir constantly until it comes to a low boil. Reduce heat and cook an additional 10 minutes until soup is thick and porridgey.

Serve hot with sprinklings of spearmint.

· WHEAT SOUP ·

HAREESEE

Another stick-to-the-ribs winter soup. *Hareesee* means "well cooked."

> **1 pound or more meaty lamb bones**
> **4 ounces lamb chunks (optional)**
> **2 quarts water**
> **1 t. salt**
>
> · · ·
>
> **¼ – 1 cup skinless whole wheat (see Note)**
>
> · · ·
>
> **¼ t. ground cinnamon**
> **¼ t. pepper**
> **1 t. salt**
> **¼ t. ground allspice (optional)**

[2 QUARTS; 6 TO 8 SERVINGS]

PREPARE lamb broth according to *labneeyee* directions (see page 104), using above amounts for lamb and water. Or simply boil bones and meat with water and 1 teaspoon salt.

Sprinkle wheat over prepared broth, using largest amount for basic *hareesee*; smallest if you prefer a thinner version. Do not stir, to avoid toughening wheat. Bring to boil. Add cinnamon, pepper, and 1 teaspoon salt (and allspice if desired). Reduce heat. Cover and simmer for 3 to 4 hours, until soup becomes thick and porridgey.

Serve hot with Arabic bread on the side.

NOTE: Aunt Celia referred to the wheat as "peeled or skinless," indicating the skins are rubbed off. If you use regular whole wheat berries, soak them for several hours and smash with pestle or break up slightly in a blender, so they can expand in the broth.

SALADS

CABBAGE SALAD, BAAKLINE STYLE

Salata-t-malfoof

120

CHICK PEA AND PARSLEY SALAD

Salata-t-hummous

121

ENDIVE WITH *KISHIK* SALAD

Hindbeh bi kishik

122

BRAIN SALAD

Salata 'n'khaa

123

. . .

As I rewrite the salad section I see that many of the salad recipes devised here or acquired in Lebanon are really just one salad, with individual tastes dictating proportions of ingredients. Salad making, like all other aspects of cooking, is extremely flexible and geared to what you have and what you like.

Summer's abundance of fresh fruits and vegetables makes it the best time to plan extensive Lebanese meals relying heavily on everything that grows in the garden – scallions, eggplants, green peppers, jumbo cabbages, thick-leaved Swiss chard, curly piquant parsley, the sturdy turnip, and on and on – always focusing on the glory of the sun-ripened, deep red, versatile, and succulent tomato. Late August triggers the start of a month of heaven for us in southern Wisconsin. It's *tabbouleh* time every day for as long as the tomatoes are good. This salad demands prime tomatoes, prime parsley, prime scallions, spearmint, lots of fresh lemon juice, and the finest olive oil you can find.

Throughout the tomato season we make salads every day, adding fresh herbs like marjoram, thyme, basil, dill, and oregano. Of course, the freshest and ripest vegetables make the finest salads. Let your creative genius and taste buds guide you to sumptuous salad making.

· TWO SIMPLE MOUNTAIN SALADS ·

SALATA KHUDRA

WISCONSIN VERSION

[2 SERVINGS]

We make a simple salad of 2 or 3 chopped whole tomatoes, 1 large slivered onion, ½ cup chopped parsley, and ⅓ to ½ cup freshly chopped spearmint (or 2 tablespoons dried), then dress it with 3 tablespoons each olive oil and either red wine vinegar or lemon juice, with salt and pepper to taste. When we're in the mood, we add garlic or feta cheese.

LEBANESE *SALATA KHUDRA*

Additional ingredients dress our Wisconsin version up more and provide variety. With ½ cup chopped purslane leaves, 1 chopped green pepper, and 1 sliced or chopped cucumber, the salad above becomes the simple mountain *salata khudra*. Garlic and red wine vinegar are used in this version. Increase oil and tartness 1 tablespoon each per additional cup vegetables and figure that each added cup will satisfy one more person.

· TOMATO, SPEARMINT, PARSLEY, · AND *BURGHUL* SALAD

TABBOULEH

Ah, *tabbouleh* . . . This is *the* traditional, national Lebanese salad, the ultimate in taste at the height of the tomato season, chief royalty among salads. What more can I say? ("You can live on *tabbouleh* alone"?)

Because we all love tomato, you'll see that the Wisconsin recipe includes a great deal more of it than the traditional Lebanese version, which centers on parsley and spearmint. Do not try making this with plastic tomatoes in the dead of winter or you'll never know *tabbouleh* in its juicy splendor.

Soaked *burghul* wheat, allspice, salt, and pepper are added to the basic vegetables and dressed liberally with olive oil and freshly squeezed lemon juice. Eaten in dripping bites, wrapped up in small freshly picked grapeleaves or romaine, and accompanied by fresh Arabic bread, this salad surpasses all others.

Pay attention to the vegetable chopping. This is a finely chopped salad, meaning some time devoted to the cutting board. The beauty of small bits of red mingling with "confettied" green and white is worth the work involved.

WISCONSIN TRADITION

¾ cup medium *burghul* (see page 6)

. . .

1 cup minced onions
1 t. ground allspice
1 t. freshly ground pepper
1 T. salt

. . .

2 cups finely chopped parsley
2 cups finely chopped scallions,
    white and green parts
4 cups finely chopped super-ripe
    tomatoes
½ cup fresh spearmint leaves,
    chopped fine
2 T. crushed dried spearmint

. . .

½ cup fresh lemon juice
½ cup olive oil

TABBOULEH OLD
COUNTRY STYLE

(This is Aunt Celia's version.)

½ cup medium or fine *burghul*
    (see page 6)

. . .

½ cup chopped onion
½ t. ground allspice
½ t. freshly ground pepper
1 – 2 t. salt

. . .

3 cups finely chopped parsley
½ cup finely chopped scallions
2 cups finely chopped tomatoes
1½ cups fresh spearmint leaves,
    chopped fine

. . .

½ cup fresh lemon juice
¾ cup olive oil

[6 TO 8 SERVINGS]

EITHER wash *burghul* according to directions on page 65, or soak in water to cover by ½ inch for 20 minutes and place in sieve to drain.

Combine minced onion with allspice, pepper, and salt. Set aside. In a large bowl, combine parsley, scallions, tomatoes, and fresh and dried spearmint. Gently fold in the soaked or rinsed wheat. Refrigerate until an hour before serving.

Stir in seasoned onion and dress with lemon and oil.

Surround salad with small romaine leaves or young grapeleaves. Use them to scoop up the salad in bites.

• SOME VARIATIONS •

Ruth advises using half curly and half Italian flat-leaved parsley. She adds 1 teaspoon ground cinnamon and only ½ teaspoon each pepper and allspice. Here is her technique for cutting tomato. With a sharp knife remove stem end of tomato. Holding tomato in left hand, sharp knife in right, with a curving sweep cut tiny wedges, rotating the tomato as you go. The wedges are pyramidal in shape and look nice in the salad. The tomato bits are added last after everything else has been tossed together.

Ruth told me that one time Sitti was having company and had no lemon juice. She substituted pomegranate juice and was given many compliments on her "new dish"!

• ORANGE LENTILS •

Omit tomatoes! Use 2 cups orange lentils, soaked overnight. Or add orange lentils in addition to tomatoes: use 2 cups chopped tomatoes with 1 cup soaked lentils. The lentils are used when tomatoes go out of season.

• CUCUMBER-PEAS ADDITION •

To basic *tabbouleh*, add 1 cup chopped cucumber and 1 cup whole fresh peas or fresh green chick peas (see page 6).

• WHEAT, TOMATO, PARSLEY, • CUCUMBER, AND *DEHEN* SALAD

TABBOULEH BI DEHEN

Aunt Alice and Aunt Libby prepared this unusual earthy mountain dish for us one hot summer day, accompanied with oven-fresh *fatayer bi flayflee* (see page 30). Lamb fat is much softer in Lebanon, so room temperature fat there would be on the soft, spreadable side. I find lamb fat here too hard to use as a "dressing," unless it is heated first. As it cools it tends to solidify again, so either serve this particular salad on a hot day or consider it as you would a hot bacon-fat type dressing. If you substituted olive oil for *dehen* and increased lemon juice to taste, you'd have a tasty salad but of a different nature.

> 1 cup medium or fine *burghul* (see page 6)
>
> • • •
>
> 1 cup green shelled chick peas (see page 6) *or* fresh green peas
> 1 cup thinly sliced cucumber
> 1 cup chopped tomatoes
> ½ cup scallions, chopped fine
> ¾ cup minced parsley
>
> • • •
>
> ½ cup *dehen* (see page 9)
> ½ cup water
> ¼ cup fresh lemon juice
> 1 – 1½ t. salt

[6 SERVINGS]

WASH *burghul* (as directed on page 65). Slightly crush chick peas with pestle. They will split; flesh will be barely smashed. (Do not smash green peas if using them instead.)

Combine cucumber, tomatoes, scallions, and parsley in bowl. Heat *dehen* and stir in water, lemon juice, and salt. Pour this dressing over salad and toss well. Serve with young tender cabbage, grapeleaves, or romaine.

• BREAD SALAD WITH POMEGRANATE •

FATTOUSH

Bread salads are exquisite because the bread soaks up the wonderful flavors of the fresh vegetables and dressing; and economical because good use is made of leftover Arabic bread. Walter's grandfather's version and Aunt Libby's are included below. The latter is more elaborate, but both are delightful.

JIDDI'S FATTOUSH

1 pomegranate

· · ·

¼ cup freshly chopped spearmint leaves *or* 2 T. dried crushed spearmint
1 – 1½ cups chopped tomatoes
1 cup peeled, quartered, and thinly sliced cucumber
1 cup minced scallions
1 cup finely chopped parsley

· · ·

¼ cup olive oil
1 t. salt
¼ t. freshly ground pepper
⅓ cup red wine vinegar

· · ·

1 loaf Arabic bread, dried (see page 20)

[4 TO 6 SERVINGS]

REMOVE whole seeds from half the pomegranate and toss in bowl with vegetables and parsley. Shake oil, salt, pepper, and vinegar together in a jar and pour over salad.

Squeeze juice from other half of pomegranate over salad and mix well. Chill.

Split bread into single layers; break into small pieces and fold into salad immediately before serving.

AUNT LIBBY'S *FATTOUSH*

Libby's recipe agrees in its ingredients down through parsley, but not in its proportions. She uses lemon juice instead of vinegar, omits pepper, and adds purslane, green pepper, onion, raw peas, garlic, sumac, and pomegranate syrup! Libby also indicated *toasted* Arabic bread, not dried.

> 1 pomegranate
>
> . . .
>
> ¼ cup freshly chopped spearmint leaves *or* 2 T. dried crushed spearmint
> 1 cup chopped tomatoes
> ½ cup peeled, quartered, and thinly sliced cucumber
> ¼ cup minced scallions
> ¾ cup finely chopped parsley
> ½ cup chopped onion
> ½ cup raw green peas
> ½ cup chopped purslane leaves
> ¼ cup chopped green pepper
>
> . . .
>
> ¼ cup olive oil
> ¼ cup fresh lemon juice
> 1 t. salt
> 1½ t. ground sumac (see page 8)
> 1½ t. pomegranate syrup (see page 7)
> 1½ large cloves garlic, crushed
>
> . . .
>
> 1 loaf Arabic bread, toasted (see page 20)

[4 TO 6 SERVINGS]

REMOVE whole seeds from half the pomegranate and toss together with remaining vegetables in a bowl. (You will *not* need to juice the remaining half pomegranate for this version.) Shake remaining ingredients (except for bread) together in a jar and pour over salad. Chill.

Fold toasted bread into salad immediately before serving.

• BASIC YOGHURT DRESSING •

Laban salads refresh your palate, cool your throat, and taste delicious! They go well with entrée dishes that normally require yoghurt on the side. Garnish these salads with a few whole spearmint leaves. A drizzle of olive oil over the salad is also good.

> ½ – 1 t. salt
> 1 – 2 T. crushed dried spearmint *or* ¼ cup fresh chopped spearmint
>   leaves
> 1 small clove garlic, crushed
> 2 cups yoghurt

[2 CUPS]

STIR salt, spearmint, and garlic into yoghurt and mix well. This dressing, eaten by itself in bites of Arabic bread, is simple and fresh.

• CUCUMBERS AND YOGHURT SALAD •

KHYAR BIL-LABAN

Always taste cucumbers before adding them to salads. Sometimes they are bitter. Choose cucumbers 1½ inches in diameter or smaller. Large seedy ones are not worth eating.

> 2 cucumbers, 6 inches long
>   · · ·
> 1 recipe basic yoghurt dressing (preceding recipe)
>   · · ·
> Fresh spearmint leaves and olive oil

[4 SERVINGS]

PEEL cucumbers and slice thin. If they are large, quarter them length-wise before slicing.

Fold cucumbers into yoghurt dressing and chill before serving. Garnish with whole spearmint leaves and a drizzle of olive oil.

• ENDIVE AND YOGHURT SALAD •

HINDBEH BIL-LABAN

Aunt Celia says, if you make the yoghurt dressing with garlic, omit the onion. She considers both the spearmint and garlic as options in this salad.

½ **head endive**
1 **large onion**

• • •

1 **recipe basic yoghurt dressing (see page 116)**

• • •

Fresh spearmint leaves and olive oil

[4 SERVINGS]

WASH endive and shake or spin dry. Chop in small, bite-sized pieces. Sliver onion in thin crescents and toss with endive. Combine with yoghurt dressing. Garnish with spearmint leaves and olive oil.

• PURSLANE AND YOGHURT SALAD •

BAKLEE BIL-LABAN

Take advantage of this common and prolific garden visitor. The succulent leaves are also used in Aunt Libby's *fattoush*.

3 cups purslane leaves

. . .

1 recipe basic yoghurt dressing (see page 116)

. . .

Fresh spearmint leaves and olive oil

[4 SERVINGS]

WASH purslane leaves well and chop into small pieces. It is not necessary to remove the stems. Mix with yoghurt dressing and chill before serving. Garnish with spearmint leaves and olive oil.

• LETTUCE, BREAD, AND YOGHURT • SALAD I

LABAN FATTOUSH I

---

1 small head romaine lettuce
1 large onion, slivered in thin crescents

. . .

1 recipe basic yoghurt dressing (see page 116), increasing yoghurt to 2½ – 3 cups

. . .

1 – 1½ loaves Arabic bread, dried (see page 20)

. . .

Fresh spearmint leaves and olive oil

[4 SERVINGS]

WASH, core, and dry lettuce. Tear or chop in 1-inch pieces. Toss slivered onion well with lettuce. Fold dressing into lettuce and onion.

Break bread into small pieces and fold into salad just before serving. Garnish with whole spearmint leaves and a drizzle of olive oil.

This is not a good salad to eat as a leftover.

· LETTUCE, BREAD, AND YOGHURT · SALAD II

LABAN FATTOUSH II

If you are serving this salad with dishes already flavored with garlic, you may wish to omit the garlic in the dressing.

> 1 cup finely chopped parsley
> ½ cup finely chopped scallions
> 1 cup peeled thinly sliced and quartered cucumber
> ½ cup fresh chopped spearmint leaves *or* 2 T. crushed dried spearmint
>
> · · ·
>
> Freshly ground pepper
> Salt
>
> · · ·
>
> 1 recipe basic yoghurt dressing (see page 116), increasing yoghurt
>   to 2½ cups
>
> · · ·
>
> 1½ large loaves Arabic bread, dried (see page 20)
> Olive oil and fresh spearmint leaves
>
> [4 to 6 servings]

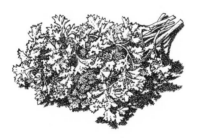

Toss together all vegetables. Add pepper and salt to taste. Fold in yoghurt dressing.

Break dried bread into small pieces and fold into salad immediately before serving. Drizzle with olive oil and garnish with fresh whole spearmint leaves.

· BEET SALAD ·

SALATA-T-SHAMANDAR

A visually rich salad with purple-red offset by bits of dark green and white. For a special treat, add a bit of pomegranate syrup.

2 cups fresh or canned beets

. . .

½ cup finely chopped onion
¾ cup finely chopped parsley

. . .

2 T. crushed dried spearmint
1 t. salt, or to taste
¼ cup olive oil
¼ cup fresh lemon juice

. . .

1 – 2 T. pomegranate syrup (see page 7) (optional)
1 small clove garlic, crushed (optional)

[3 TO 4 SERVINGS]

IF using fresh beets, wash and stem; boil or steam until tender; then skin, slice, and dice in small pieces. Cut canned beets into small pieces. Toss with onion and parsley.

Dress with spearmint, salt, oil, lemon juice, optional pomegranate syrup, and garlic. Toss salad well and chill before serving.

· CABBAGE SALAD, BAAKLINE STYLE ·

SALATA-T-MALFOOF

Tucked up in the mountains of Lebanon, the village of Baakline has been "home" to generations of Hamadys. Cousin Maya prepared this salad for us.

For variation, pit and quarter twelve Greek olives and add to salad. A pinch of cayenne pepper adds zest.

½ head cabbage, chopped or shredded
1 cup chopped tomato
½ cup chopped onion
½ cup chopped parsley
¼ cup chopped scallions

· · ·

3 T. olive oil
3 T. fresh lemon juice
1 t. salt, or to taste
1 clove garlic, crushed

· · ·

1 T. crushed dried spearmint

[4 SERVINGS]

Toss vegetables together and chill. Dress with oil, lemon juice, salt, and garlic. Sprinkle spearmint over salad before serving.

· CHICK PEA AND PARSLEY SALAD ·

SALATA-T-HUMMOUS

AUNT HAJAR'S SALAD

½ cup dry chick peas, soaked overnight (see page 72)

· · ·

½ cup finely chopped onion
1 cup finely chopped parsley

· · ·

¼ cup olive oil
¼ cup fresh lemon juice
¼ cup chick pea juice
½ t. salt, or more
1 small clove garlic, crushed (optional)

[3 TO 4 SMALL SERVINGS]

Cook chick peas in soaking water 1 – 1¼ hours, until tender. You should have 1½ cups cooked. Drain, reserving ¼ cup cooking juice for salad dressing. Combine chick peas with onion and parsley, tossing well. Dress with oil, lemon and cooking juices, salt, and optional garlic.

Chill before serving.

• VARIATION •

Cousin Leila adds these remarks: "You can make it with chopped tomatoes, fried pine nuts (on top), and 1 tablespoon of *tahini* added to the dressing."

• ENDIVE WITH *KISHIK* SALAD •

HINDBEH BI KISHIK

An unusual salad. *Kishik* adds some tartness but, more importantly, an almost cheesy flavor.

> **1 small head endive**
> **1 large onion, slivered in thin crescents**
> . . .
> **½ cup *kishik* (see page 6)**
> . . .
> **¼ – ⅓ cup fresh lemon juice**
> **½ cup olive oil**
> **1 t. salt, or to taste**

[4 TO 6 SERVINGS]

Wash endive and shake or spin dry. Tear carefully into small pieces. Toss with slivered onion.

Sprinkle *kishik* over salad and dress with lemon, oil, and salt. Toss well and chill 30 minutes before serving.

· BRAIN SALAD ·

SALATA 'N'KHAA

Brains are delicate, subtle, and rich — hard to come by but worth the search.

    4 lamb brains
    2 cups water
    1 lemon, sliced
    1 small onion, sliced
    ¼ t. ground cinnamon
    ½ t. salt
    · · ·
    3 T. fresh lemon juice
    3 T. olive oil
    ½ t. salt
    1 small clove garlic, crushed
    · · ·
    2 T. minced parsley
    Lemon wedges

[4 SERVINGS]

REMOVE membrane from brains and wash carefully in cold water. Place in large saucepan and cover with water. Add lemon, onion, cinnamon, and ½ teaspoon salt. Simmer 15 to 20 minutes, until just tender.

Remove brains from bouillon and let cool. Slice or chop and place in serving dish. Mix together lemon, olive oil, ½ teaspoon salt, and garlic and use to dress brains. Sprinkle with parsley and serve with wedges of lemon and Arabic bread.

· IX ·

VEGETABLE
DISHES

STEAMED VEGETABLES WITH *TARATOOR*
129

STEAMED VEGETABLES WITH GARLIC, LEMON, AND OIL
130

DEEP-FRIED VEGETABLES WITH *TARATOOR* ON THE SIDE
130

ARTICHOKES IN OIL
Ardishawki bzeit
130

EGYPTIAN FAVA BEANS IN OIL
Fool moudammas
132

GREEN BEANS WITH TOMATO AND ONION
Loubieh bzeit
132

CAULIFLOWER FRITTERS
Qarnabeet maklee
133

KOOSA OR ZUCCHINI FRITTERS
Koosa maklee
134

EGGPLANT WITH TOMATO, ONION, AND CHICK PEAS
Menazzaleh
135

COLD STUFFED GRAPELEAVES
Warak areesh bzeit
137

COLD STUFFED SWISS CHARD
Mahshi silq bzeit
139

LENTILS AND RICE
Mujaddarah
139

. . .

W ITH the abundance of fresh produce available in Lebanon, it is not surprising to find a similar abundance of recipes for salads, stews, stuffed vegetables, and side dishes stemming from the garden. Meat is expensive everywhere and not always available. *Dehen,* somewhat like a meaty shortening made from lamb suet, fried lamb pieces, and spices, is often used to give dishes a light meat flavor without the expense or bulk of meat. The mountain people base many of their meals on fruit and vegetables, supplemented by yoghurt and bread. Rice, cracked wheat, and legumes such as chick peas, lentils, and dried beans are relied on heavily as a cheap and accessible protein source.

I didn't know anything about protein complements when I was in Lebanon. On our return to the States I discovered that all kinds of protein-complement relationships existed in the Lebanese cuisine. Dishes with beans or chick peas and cracked wheat, or rice and chick peas, or even the acclaimed *hummous* – chick peas and sesame seed paste dip – provided complete proteins, especially when served, as most of them were, with yoghurt. Since it is not the purpose of this book to discuss in depth the nature of protein or nutrition, I merely want to point out the natural potential and excellence within the Lebanese regime, which could easily be referred to as primarily vegetarian, without proclaiming it *just* that.

Many recipes in this section are simple and straightforward. Sometimes vegetables are just steamed and served with either a lemon-oil-garlic dressing or a *taratoor* sauce made from sesame seed paste blended with water, lemon, and garlic. A few more complex recipes, such as cold stuffed grapeleaves, *kibbeh lakhteen*, or *lakhteen bi hummous*, demand time and patience but are well worth the effort. Self-declared pumpkin-hater friends of ours devoured both of the latter dishes to their delight, with full knowledge of what they were eating! You may find that these time-consuming recipes are a great deal of fun if you invite your friends over early for a long afternoon of cooking and tomfoolery. The washing, chopping, sorting, frying, and stuffing go quickly with many hands. When Walter and I would go to Aunt Alice's house for a "cooking bee," we'd end up spending half the day in the kitchen preparing the food, albeit at a leisurely rate, between bites of *kibbeh* or *hummous* and sips of simmering yoghurt sauce that waited for pleated dumplings stuffed with chick peas and onion. The rest of the day we spent on the veranda – yes, eating *tabbouleh bi dehen*, and warm fresh *fatayer bi flayflee*, and occasionally squeezing pits out of home-cured, home-grown succulent olives, with a bite of Arabic bread.

But I see I am drifting from the business at hand, which is tomatoes. Because they play such an important role in this section and those on stews and stuffed specialties, I want to inject a few biased words on the subject.

ABOUT TOMATOES AND COOKING

Nothing compares to a *vine ripe* tomato when this succulent delicious fruit is discussed. In season, it makes sense to use a lot of them frequently. Any surplus is easy to can up for those cold bleak months of winter. Since tomatoes are bottled up at the peak of their ripeness and sweetness, the home-canned variety still beats the plastic "fresh greenhouse tomato" sold during the siege of dormant months. In Wisconsin, our prime tomato time is usually from the end of August through September, which means about one month of really good eating. That leaves eleven dry months and may explain why I've indicated canned tomatoes instead of fresh ones for recipes which are to be baked or simmered. Should you be fortunate enough to have easy access to good ripe fruit all the time, by all means use the fresh for everything. Simply scald them, remove the stems and skins, and crush them in a measure to arrive at the amount required for the recipe.

• STEAMED VEGETABLES •
WITH *TARATOOR*

One of the simplest and most delicious ways to prepare any given vegetable is to steam it and serve it hot or cold covered with a mantle of garlicky *taratoor* sauce. Or, if you prefer, serve the *taratoor* on the side and let your guests do the honors.

Another simple method involves steaming the vegetable briefly, drying it out a bit, and quickly deep-fat frying until golden. These tender morsels are then dipped in *taratoor* and eaten with Arabic bread.

Any leftover juices from steamed vegetables can be used in soup stock, gravies, or sauces.

Below are those vegetables commonly steamed.

> **Broccoli, broken into flowerets**
> **Cauliflower, in small flowerets**
> **Swiss chard stems, in bite-sized pieces**
> **String green or wax beans, whole or broken**

Additional suggestions, not traditional but good (add your own, too!):

> **Carrots**
> **Celery**
> **Asparagus spears**
> **Brussels sprouts**
> **· · ·**
>
> **1 recipe *taratoor* (see page 59)**
> **Parsley and paprika**

[1 POUND SERVES 4]

BRING ½ inch water to boil in heavy saucepan. Place washed vegetables in steamer basket or on rack over water. Cover pan tightly and steam until just tender. Timing will vary according to vegetable—watch closely. Pour *taratoor* sauce over hot vegetables and serve immediately. Garnish with sprigs of parsley and paprika and accompany with Arabic bread.

If you decide to serve this at room temperature, blanket with *taratoor* after vegetables are fully cooled, or just before serving, so the sauce doesn't separate.

• STEAMED VEGETABLES WITH GARLIC, LEMON, • AND OIL

Pour lemon dressing (see page 58) over hot or cold steamed vegetables. This is a marinade-type sauce, so you *can* cover the vegetables with it while they are hot and for as long as you like.

• DEEP-FRIED VEGETABLES • WITH *TARATOOR* ON THE SIDE

Traditionally both cauliflower and eggplant are deep fried, then served with *taratoor* on the side.

Potatoes, *koosa* or zucchini, broccoli, pumpkin, carrot strips, and even parsley could also be deep fried. Treat *koosa* like eggplant, steam carrots and broccoli like cauliflower, and deep fry potatoes or pumpkin like french fries.

Cauliflower (Break in small flowerets; steam for 3 – 4 minutes;
dry out 5 – 10 minutes before deep-fat frying.)
Eggplant (Peel; slice in ½-inch rounds; salt lightly and place in colander
to drain for 30 minutes; pat dry.)
1 recipe *taratoor* (see page 59)

[1 POUND SERVES 4]

READ about deep-fat frying on page 11. Deep fry vegetables at 360° to 375° until golden to darkish brown. Drain on absorbent cloth or paper. Serve with *taratoor* sauce and Arabic bread.

• ARTICHOKES IN OIL •

ARDISHAWKI BZEIT

Cousin Maya Hamady prepared these in an elaborate and delicious *maza*, in August 1972. Artichokes are plentiful in the Middle East, growing wild like giant thistles all over the arid land.

As part of *maza*, these stuffed artichoke bottoms, also referred to as "cups," are lovely and delicious. They can be prepared quite quickly if you use artichoke bottoms canned or pickled in oil. I tried the fresh method, steaming the whole artichokes in a pressure cooker until tender and then peeling off the multitudes of leaves to reveal the scrawny crowns. Perhaps I bought a puny batch, for the bottoms were substantially smaller than the usual pickled variety; to avoid the time, work, and waste involved, I highly recommend buying your artichoke bottoms prepared.

> ¼ cup olive oil
> 12 – 16 artichoke bottoms or "cups," bottled in oil or canned
>   . . .
> 2 carrots, peeled
> 1 cup finely chopped onions
> 1 – 2 cloves garlic, crushed
>   . . .
> ¾ cup water
> ½ t. salt
>   . . .
> 1½ t. flour
> 2 T. fresh lemon juice
>   . . .
> 2 T. chopped parsley

[3 TO 4 SERVINGS]

IN a skillet heat olive oil over moderately high heat and brown artichoke bottoms quickly; set them aside. Quarter carrots lengthwise and chop fine. Add carrots, onions, and garlic to oil and sauté 5 minutes. Add ¾ cup water and simmer 10 minutes longer, until tender. Stir in salt and return artichoke bottoms to skillet. Simmer 5 to 10 minutes for flavors to blend.

Remove artichoke bottoms with slotted spoon and arrange them on serving platter. With slotted spoon, remove carrot and onion mixture and place a generous tablespoon in each artichoke cup.

Blend flour with lemon juice to form a smooth paste and stir into pan juices. Cook a few minutes until sauce thickens. (If necessary, add a few tablespoons water.) Stir in parsley.

Pour sauce over stuffed artichokes and cool to room temperature before serving.

• EGYPTIAN FAVA BEANS IN OIL •

FOOL MOUDAMMAS

For greater variety of color and texture, add ⅓ cup each finely chopped onion and parsley as you are dressing the beans. Egyptian fava beans, to the best of my knowledge, are smaller beans than the horsey fava beans found in the States. Pinto beans are acceptable as a substitute.

1½ cups dry Egyptian fava beans

· · ·

½ cup fresh lemon juice
½ cup olive oil, plus oil for drizzling
5 large cloves garlic, crushed
2 t. salt
¼ t. freshly ground pepper

· · ·

Parsley
2 T. cooked chick peas (see pages 72 – 74)

[3 TO 4 CUPS; 6 TO 8 SERVINGS]

RINSE beans and soak overnight in 3 cups water. Then add 1 cup more water, cover, and simmer 3 to 4 hours, until beans are very tender. Add water to beans if necessary. Skins may be tougher than interior – perfectly natural for fava beans.

Drain beans and dress with lemon juice, oil, garlic, salt, and pepper. Drizzle with additional olive oil and garnish with sprigs of parsley and whole chick peas. Serve warm or at room temperature with Arabic bread and bits of sweet onion or scallion.

• GREEN BEANS WITH TOMATO • AND ONION

LOUBIEH BZEIT

This is another simple dish that produced a slight family controversy, with the tomato and garlic as culprits. Ruth says garlic isn't traditional and likes to dissolve her onion by simmering it in a little water before adding the fried beans and tomato. Aunt Libby and Aunt Celia (and for that matter, the major Lebanese contingent) like *loubieh* with a lot less tomato than I use — 1 pint to our quart, deleting tomato paste completely. Here is my favorite version.

1 pound green beans

. . .

1 clove garlic, crushed or whole
1 cup onions, chopped or slivered in thin crescents
¼ cup olive oil

. . .

1 quart canned tomatoes
6 ounces tomato paste
Pinch sugar
1 t. salt
Parsley

[1½ TO 2 QUARTS; 6 TO 8 SERVINGS OR MORE]

Wash and stem beans, if using fresh; or slightly thaw frozen beans, enough to break them apart.

Crush the garlic; if you want a less garlicky taste, use the whole clove and remove it after frying the onions. Brown onions in oil with garlic until they are light brown around the edges and translucent. Stir in green beans and fry them 5 minutes. Then add tomatoes, tomato paste, sugar, and salt.

Bring to simmer, partially cover pan, and cook slowly for about an hour, until sauce is thick and beans very tender.

Cool to room temperature before serving. Garnish with fresh parsley and serve with Arabic bread.

A delicious variation to this recipe is okra with tomato and onion (*bamieh bzeit*), in which okra is substituted for green beans.

• CAULIFLOWER FRITTERS •

QARNABEET MAKLEE

Also referred to in the family as *ijjee*, the cauliflower fritters are delicate, delicious, and very suitable for serving to a group — they will be eaten up quickly (which is exactly what you want). The batter with sumac is unusual and pleasing; that with cinnamon and allspice, more traditional. There are more fritter recipes using other vegetables in this chapter.

1 large head cauliflower

Wash and core cauliflower. Break into bite-sized flowerets and steam for 4 to 5 minutes. Set aside to dry and cool while making batter.

CINNAMON-ALLSPICE BATTER	SUMAC BATTER
	1 cup minced scallions or dry onions
½ cup minced onion	**1 cup finely chopped parsley**
½ cup finely chopped parsley	**¾ cup fresh spearmint leaves** *or*
½ t. ground cinnamon	**3 T. dried spearmint**
½ t. ground allspice	**1 T. ground sumac (see page 8)**
1 t. salt	**1 t. salt**
¼ t. freshly ground pepper	**¼ t. freshly ground pepper**
· · ·	· · ·
3 large eggs	**5 eggs**
¾ cup flour	**¾ cup flour**
½ cup water	· · ·
· · ·	

2 quarts vegetable oil for frying
Lemon wedges

[6 TO 8 SERVINGS]

Follow same mixing procedure for both batters; the eggs in sumac batter make up for water's absence. Mix onion, parsley, and seasonings together. Beat eggs well. Blend in flour (and water) and beat until smooth. Add onion mixture and stir to blend.

Dip flowerets in batter and deep fry at 375° until golden to dark brown. Drain on absorbent cloth or paper. Keep warm in 200° oven until all fritters are ready to serve.

Serve hot with wedges of lemon and Arabic bread.

• *KOOSA* OR ZUCCHINI FRITTERS •

KOOSA MAKLEE

Koosa or zucchini fritters make a light tasty lunch, solving the leftover (pulp-from-hollowed-out) summer squash problem, or simply that of *what to do* with all that zucchini. The *koosa*/zucchini dip, in the *maza* chapter, offers another idea.

> **Vegetable oil for frying**
>
> · · ·
>
> **4 eggs**
> **8 – 9 T. flour**
> **1½ t. salt**
> **¼ t. freshly ground pepper**
>
> · · ·
>
> **1 cup chopped fresh spearmint leaves *or* 4 T. dried crushed spearmint**
> **1 cup finely chopped parsley**
> **2½ cups grated or finely chopped squash (Unless you're using pulp,**
> **do not peel squash; the green is delightful.)**

[4 SERVINGS]

HEAT 1 inch oil in skillet over medium high heat. Beat eggs; stir in flour, salt, and pepper. Gently fold mint, parsley, and squash into flour mixture until consistency of batter is uniform.

Drop by large tablespoons into hot oil and fry until medium to golden brown. Drain on absorbent paper and keep warm in a 200° oven until all the fritters have finished cooking.

Good with yoghurt or salad made with yoghurt.

· EGGPLANT WITH TOMATO, ONION, ·
AND CHICK PEAS

MENAZZALEH

When eggplants are in season, try frying up a lot of eggplants at one time. Freeze the slices on a tray and package them once frozen. All winter you can make this dish without smoking up your kitchen; place slightly thawed pieces in dish and cover with hot sauce. Bake as usual.

Thanks to Aunt Jenny and Uncle Sam, who make a mean *menazzaleh*.

Scant ½ cup dry chick peas (see page 6)

. . .

1 large round eggplant (at least 1 pound)
Salt

. . .

¼ cup olive oil
1½ – 2 cups chopped onions

. . .

1 t. salt
6 ounces tomato paste
1 quart tomatoes, canned or fresh peeled

. . .

½ cup olive or vegetable oil for frying

[6 SERVINGS]

RINSE, sort, and soak chick peas overnight. Simmer next day in soaking water for 60 minutes, until just tender. Drain before adding to tomatoes. Peel eggplant and cut in half lengthwise. Slice each half in half-moons ½ inch thick. Salt lightly and place in colander to drain for 30 minutes.

Heat ¼ cup olive oil and fry onions until light brown around the edges. Stir in 1 teaspoon salt, tomato paste, and drained chick peas. Cut tomatoes in quarters and add to pan. Simmer mixture uncovered for 20 to 30 minutes, until sauce thickens.

Pat eggplant pieces dry and fry in small amount of oil until brown on both sides, adding oil as needed. You may prefer to brush eggplant slices lightly with oil and broil until medium brown on both sides. Drain on absorbent cloth or paper.

Put half the sauce into an 8-by-14-inch casserole and arrange eggplant over. Cover with remaining sauce. Bake at 350° for 20 to 30 minutes so flavors blend.

Serve at room temperature garnished with parsley and accompanied by the ever-present *khubuz arabee*, Arabic bread!

• AUNT LIBBY'S *MENAZZALEH* •

Here is an excellent variation, using split chick peas and garlic; she also prefers lots of slivered onions.

1 cup dry chick peas, soaked overnight (see page 72)

   .   .   .

2 large round eggplants
Salt
Salt
1 cup vegetable oil

   .   .   .

3 cups or more onions, slivered in thin crescents
6 – 8 large whole cloves garlic
3 cups water

   .   .   .

½ – 1 cup water
6 ounces tomato paste
1 t. salt

[8 TO 10 SERVINGS]

SKIN and split soaked chick peas. Peel and quarter eggplants lengthwise. Cut each quarter into 3 or 4 lengthwise wedges. Salt lightly and place in colander to drain 30 minutes. Heat oil and fry eggplant until wedges are very dark brown on all sides. Add more oil as necessary. Drain on absorbent cloth or paper. Pour off all but 2 tablespoons oil.

Brown onions in remaining oil until soft and light brown. Drain chick peas and add with garlic to onions. Fry 5 minutes longer. Stir in 3 cups water, cover pan, and cook 30 minutes, until chick peas are very tender. Add ½ to 1 cup water and blend in tomato paste and salt.

Arrange fried eggplant over top and simmer gently 15 to 20 minutes to blend flavors and thicken sauce. Cool to room temperature and serve with Arabic bread.

• COLD STUFFED GRAPELEAVES •

WARAK AREESH BZEIT

This is traditional delightful Middle Eastern fare, served as *maza* or part of the main meal. Hot stuffed grapeleaves (*mahshi warak areesh*), filled with meat, rice, and tomato, could be considered the winter counterpart of this spiced lentil-and-rice version.

Aunt Libby serves grapeleaves with hot chili peppers. Sometimes a layer of green pepper is placed over a layer of unstuffed grapeleaves on the bottom of the pan, then the rolled leaves are placed over these. Or small green peppers are stuffed with the filling and cooked along with the grapeleaves.

1 quart pickled grapeleaves, or use fresh (see Note)

. . .

Scant ½ cup dry chick peas, soaked overnight (see page 72)

. . .

1 cup raw short-grain rice
1 cup lentils

. . .

1¼ t. ground cinnamon
1 t. ground allspice
1 T. salt
½ t. freshly ground pepper
1½ cups finely chopped onions

. . .

1 cup chopped parsley
½ cup fresh lemon juice
½ cup olive oil

. . .

¼ cup lemon juice
Lemon wedges

[100 SMALL OR 50 LARGE GRAPELEAVES; 10 OR MORE SERVINGS]

CAREFULLY wash pickled grapeleaves and drape them over a colander to drain. Split and skin soaked chick peas. Cook in soaking water 20 minutes, until just tender. Soak rice in 1 cup water for 30 minutes; drain.

Cook lentils in 2½ cups water for 30 minutes, until just tender; drain.

Mix together cinnamon, allspice, salt, pepper, and onions. Stir in parsley, ½ cup lemon juice, olive oil, and soaked rice. Add cooked lentils and chick peas.

Stuff, roll, and arrange grapeleaves according to recipe for hot stuffed grapeleaves (see page 153) and cover with inverted plate. Add enough water to cover plate. Cover pot and bring to boil. Reduce heat and cook for 1 hour; during last 30 minutes add ¼ cup lemon juice to pot.

Cool grapeleaves to room temperature before removing from pot. Serve with wedges of lemon. Leaves are beautiful when placed in an oiled mold and turned out onto a platter. If desired, drizzle with olive oil.

VARIATION: Use *tabbouleh* ingredients for the stuffing, but substitute rice for the *burghul* (see page 110).

NOTE: If you use fresh grapeleaves, blanch them briefly by steaming them a minute or two until they are limp; this will make them easier to handle when stuffing.

• COLD STUFFED SWISS CHARD •

MAHSHI SILQ BZEIT

The texture of chard is not as leathery as that of the grapeleaf so you may have to take more care working with these leaves. Not as common as stuffed grapeleaves but an acceptable alternative. Meat and rice stuffing (see page 153) may also be used with chard leaves.

> **15 – 20 large Swiss chard leaves**
>
>   •   •   •
>
> **1 recipe *tabbouleh*, Old Country style (see page 110), replacing *burghul***
>   **with equal amount of short-grain rice, soaked in water**
>   **to cover for ½ hour and drained, and omitting allspice**
>
>   •   •   •
>
> **Water or tomato juice**

[ABOUT 50 ROLLS; 8 TO 10 SERVINGS]

CAREFULLY wash chard. To make handling easier, place wet leaves in dry pot and steam a few seconds (no more or they will become too limp). Split chard lengthwise and remove central vein and stem. Save stems and veins to put on the bottom of the pot. Cut into workable pieces – 3 by 5 inches or so. Place smooth side down and put several teaspoons filling on lower third across width of leaf. Roll up like a cigar.

Place in pan as you would grapeleaves (see page 153), one layer east-west, next layer north-south. Cover top layer with a chard leaf or two and top with an inverted plate.

Pour enough water or tomato juice over stuffed chard to cover plate. Cover pot and simmer 1 hour. Cool to room temperature before unpacking pan.

Good with wedges of lemon.

• LENTILS AND RICE •

MUJADDARAH

This rich but mild lentil dish complements hot spicy food superbly. It is the Middle Eastern counterpart of the East Indian *dal*. Common accompaniments are scallions and radishes, along with the traditional pickled turnip.

Sitti told Ruth that her father-in-law, Amin Hattoum Himadeh (Walter's great-grandfather, who died at 117), said one should eat dishes prepared with olive oil when they were at room temperature – if you ate them hot, they would make you dizzy! Ruth adds that Sitti did not use pepper in this dish.

⅓ cup olive oil
2 cups finely chopped onions

· · ·

1½ cups water

· · ·

1 T. salt
¼ t. freshly ground pepper, or to taste
¼ cup raw short-grain rice
2 cups lentils
1½ quarts water

· · ·

Freshly ground pepper
Arabic bread
Scallions
Radishes
Pickled turnips (see page 41)
Lemon wedges
Olive oil (optional)

[2 QUARTS; 8 SERVINGS]

IN a large pan heat olive oil and brown onions over high heat, stirring constantly so onions don't burn. Fry them 15 to 20 minutes, until they shrivel and turn a very dark even brown. They will, in fact, be on the verge of turning black, which does not mean they are scorched or burned.

Remove pan from heat and stir in ½ cup water; stir vigorously. The water will be absorbed almost immediately and onions will mush up. Add ½ cup more water and return to heat. Simmer until water is almost absorbed, and repeat a third time. Onions should be well puréed by now.

Stir in salt, pepper, rice, and lentils, and add 1½ quarts water. Bring to boil, reduce heat, cover, and simmer 1 hour until consistency becomes very, very thick, almost pasty. Remember it will thicken as it cools.

Pour into a serving dish and cool to room temperature before serving.

Serve with freshly ground pepper, Arabic bread, scallions, radishes, pickled turnips (see page 41), and wedges of lemon. Drizzle with olive oil, if desired.

• FRIED POTATOES WITH SUMAC SAUCE •

BATTATTA BI MARQUET SUMMAK

An unusual sauce. These potatoes would go best with a plain meat entrée — *shish kebab, kibbeh,* or broiled *kefta* — fish, or chicken.

> **2 T. ground sumac (see page 8)**
> **2 cups hot or boiling water**
> **1 large clove garlic, crushed**
> **Juice of 1 lemon**
> **1 t. salt, or to taste**
> **· · ·**
> **Vegetable oil for frying**
> **4 large potatoes**

[4 SERVINGS]

SOAK sumac in water several minutes. Stir in garlic, lemon juice, and salt. Heat 1 inch oil in skillet. Peel potatoes and cut in ⅛-inch slices. Fry half of them in hot oil until brown and crispy. As they are finished, place them immediately in sumac sauce.

Fry second batch of potatoes. When they are ready, remove first batch from sauce to serving bowl and keep warm in oven. Soak second batch in sumac sauce for a few minutes and serve both batches with additional sauce on the side.

• PUMPKIN CROQUETTES •

KIBBEH LAKHTEEN

These delectable croquettes have a thin pumpkin-wheat outer shell which is slightly sweet, due to the nature of pumpkin. In combination with any of the three fillings, they are an absolute taste sensation and indicate the fine art of mountain cookery.

Make one recipe of each of the three fillings, or triple an individual filling for this amount of dough. Since these take some time to prepare, you may want to make the fillings ahead. Your efforts will be well rewarded.

Aunt Adelle, who lives in the States, is famous for this dish. Her dough recipe is given below.

DOUGH

1 cup boiling water
2 cups medium *burghul* (see page 6)
. . .
2 cups or 1 pound mashed puréed pumpkin
1 t. salt
¼ t. freshly ground pepper
2 t. ground cumin

[30 TO 35 CROQUETTES]

IN a large mixing bowl pour boiling water over *burghul.* Stir in pumpkin, salt, pepper, and cumin.

Knead dough hard for 10 minutes, squeezing with hands to develop the gluten in the wheat. Dough should become somewhat elastic and pliable so it holds together as the required shapes are formed.

Keep hands moistened with water so dough does not stick to your fingers; divide dough into 30 to 35 balls and poke a finger into the center of each to form a cavity and a thin shell of dough. Fill with 1 tablespoon filling and pinch end shut.

For each filling, form croquettes into a different shape. The traditional ones are: small flat round patties, round balls, and tapered footballs. After filling and shaping croquettes, chill them for several hours. This makes them easier to fry. Deep fry 2 or 3 at a time in hot (375°) oil until golden brown all over. Drain on rack or toweling and keep warm in 200° oven until they have finished cooking. Serve hot.

I. CHICK PEA FILLING

⅓ cup dry chick peas, rinsed, sorted, and soaked overnight
    in 1⅓ cups water
. . .
⅔ cup finely chopped onion
3 T. *dehen* (see page 9)
Salt

[¾ CUP: FILLS 10 TO 12 CROQUETTES]

Drain soaked chick peas, saving soaking water to cook them in. Skin and split chick peas as directed on page 73. Cook in soaking water until tender, about 20 minutes.

While chick peas cook, fry onion in *dehen* until light brown and soft, 10 to 15 minutes. Crush cooked chick peas slightly, using a mortar and pestle. Add them to onion, with salt to taste.

Simmer 5 minutes and cool before filling.

II. *DEHEN-KISHIK* FILLING

1 cup chopped onions
½ cup *dehen* (see page 9)
⅓ cup *kishik* (see page 6)

[¾ CUP; FILLS 10 TO 12 CROQUETTES]

Brown onions in *dehen* until light brown and soft. Stir in *kishik* and fry 5 minutes. Turn frequently so *kishik* does not burn. Mixture will be stiff.

III. POTATO-*DEHEN* FILLING

2½ T. *dehen* (see page 9)
¾ cup mashed potatoes
Salt

[¾ CUP; FILLS 10 TO 12 CROQUETTES]

Melt *dehen* and stir into potatoes. Mix well and salt to taste.

· PUMPKIN WITH *TAHINI*, CHICK PEAS, · AND ONION

LAKHTEEN BI HUMMOUS

Aunt Libby and Ruth made this delicious, unusual pumpkin dish for us. For tartness in the sauce, Ruth prefers cider vinegar, which we usually use as well. Libby and Walter prefer lemon juice, but both are good. Use the larger amount of chick peas indicated if you use the lemon juice. If pumpkin is unavailable, try substituting hubbard or butternut squash.

⅔ cup – 1 cup dry chick peas, rinsed, sorted, and soaked
    overnight in 3 – 4 cups water

. . .

1 small pumpkin (2½ – 3 pounds)
Vegetable or olive oil for frying

. . .

2 T. olive oil
1½ cups onions, chopped or slivered in thin crescents

. . .

1 – 1½ cups water

. . .

⅔ cup *tahini* (see page 8)
2 cups water
1 T. salt
1 cup fresh lemon juice or cider vinegar

[2 QUARTS; 8 TO 10 SERVINGS]

SPLIT and skin chick peas, following directions on page 73, and set aside. Wash off pumpkin. Cut out lid. Split into quarters and scrape off seeds and membranes. Slice pumpkin in vertical strips 2 inches wide and cut off peel. Cut slices into 1-by-2-inch chunks and weigh out 2 pounds' worth. (Extra pumpkin can be fried separately for immediate and delicious consumption, or frozen – though the firm texture gets lost in this process.)

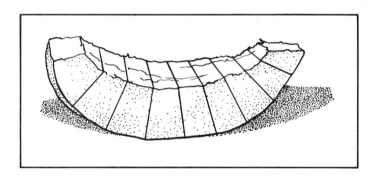

In deep skillet, heat 1 inch vegetable or olive oil. (Vegetable is fine because you'll get the olive oil flavor later with the onions, but if you're feeling extravagant, fry the pumpkin in olive oil, too.) Brown pumpkin chunks a few at a time until medium-dark brown on all sides. Drain on rack or paper. When pumpkin is finished, pour off oil and add 2 tablespoons olive oil to skillet. Pumpkin may also be deep fried, 12 to 15 per batch, at 375° – read page 11 for helpful information on deep-fat frying.

Fry onions until brown around the edges and golden all over. Add skinned split chick peas to onions and fry slowly 5 to 10 minutes longer. Add water: 1 cup for smaller amount of chick peas, 1½ cups for larger. Cover pan and simmer 20 to 25 minutes, until chick peas are tender.

Put *tahini* in mixing bowl and slowly stir in 2 cups water. Then beat in salt and either lemon juice or cider vinegar. Once chick peas are tender, place browned pumpkin over them and simmer 5 minutes. Then stir in *tahini* sauce and simmer until it thickens and pumpkin is completely tender, about 10 minutes.

Serve at room temperature with Arabic bread. Sauce will be quite thick when it has cooled.

· SPINACH AND OIL ·

SABANEKH BZEIT

Via the grapevine, we hear that Aunt Wadia served this dish garnished with crispy browned onions. The garnish definitely makes the spinach extra special.

> **1 cup chopped onions**
> **3 T. olive oil**
> **1 t. salt**
>   .   .   .
> **1 pound fresh spinach**
>   .   .   .
> **1½ cups onions, slivered in thin crescents**
> **3 T. olive oil**
> **Lemon wedges**

[3 TO 4 SERVINGS]

SAUTE onions in 3 tablespoons olive oil until light brown and stir in salt. Briefly steam spinach: wash leaves and place in covered pot over medium heat until they wilt. Arrange spinach over onions and cover pan. Simmer 10 to 15 minutes.

While spinach cooks, brown the all-important, non-optional onion slivers in 3 tablespoons olive oil until they are wonderfully browned and crispy. Arrange over spinach in serving dish and surround with wedges of lemon.

Serve warm or at room temperature.

· SPINACH AND RICE ·

SABANEKH WA ROZ

Good anytime. Everybody seems to enjoy this dish.

1 pound fresh spinach *or* **1 ten-ounce package frozen spinach**

· · ·

1 cup finely chopped onions
2 T. olive oil

· · ·

1 t. salt
1 cup water

· · ·

½ cup raw short-grain rice
Lemon wedges

[4 SERVINGS]

WASH, drain, and chop fresh spinach, or thaw frozen spinach enough to separate and chop it. Using 1-quart saucepan, sauté onions in hot oil until pale yellow and lightly browned around the edges. Add salt and water.

Bring to simmer and stir in spinach and rice. Return to simmer, cover pan, and cook slowly for 35 to 40 minutes, until rice is sticky and glutinous. Stir occasionally.

Oil a 3- to 4-cup mold and pack spinach and rice in firmly. Cool to room temperature. Unmold and surround with wedges of lemon. Yoghurt is good on the side.

· *BURGHUL* WITH TOMATO ·

BURGHUL BI BANADOURA

Jiddi, Walter's grandfather, liked this dish with *koosa* in season (wash 1 or 2 *koosa* or zucchini and slice in ½-inch rounds; add at the same time as *burghul*).

For variation, substitute raw rice for *burghul*. The meat version of this recipe can be found on page 216.

NOTE: Strict vegetarians can substitute olive oil for *dehen* in this recipe.

⅓ cup *dehen* (see page 9)
1 cup or more chopped onions

   · · ·

¼ t. ground cinnamon
1 t. salt
¼ t. freshly ground pepper, or to taste
2½ cups stewed tomatoes

   · · ·

⅔ – 1 cup large *burghul* (Sitti's recipe called for ⅔ cup *burghul*, but Aunt Adelle used 1 cup.)

[4 SERVINGS]

MELT *dehen* and fry onions until translucent and light brown around edges. Add cinnamon, salt, pepper, and tomatoes. Bring to low boil. Sprinkle in *burghul*; gently push down with back of spoon until it is all moistened. Cover pan and simmer for 30 to 35 minutes, until *burghul* is fully swelled and soft. If you use the smaller amount of *burghul*, the consistency will be more porridgey.

Eat with freshly ground pepper in bites of Arabic bread while steamy hot.

· X ·

STUFFED VEGETABLES

STUFFED PICKLED *KOOSA* OR ZUCCHINI
167

ARTICHOKES IN CASSEROLE,
WITH TOMATO OR WHITE SAUCE
Ardishawki mahshi
168

POTATO PIE
Saneeyeh-t-battatta
169

. . .

T HE Middle East is famous for stuffed vegetables, most notably the grape-leaf. There are few things as lovely as a turned-out mold of shiny grape-leaves accented with a few stuffed green peppers or zucchini

— unless you consider a platter of black cylindrical eggplants floating on a sea of yoghurt...
— or a mound of crinkle-ribbed cabbage rolls stuffed with rice and meat and speckled with spearmint, smelling of garlic...
— or a raft of zucchini boats stuffed with meat and pine nuts discreetly surrounded by tomato or white sauce.

There are endless variations using vegetables and basic sauces. For instance, sliced green pepper may be scattered over the top of stuffed eggplant or *koosa* before the sauce is added. Or eggplant and *koosa* can be sliced in rounds, then fried and layered up, using meat and pine nut filling. Garlic is used lovingly, but *not* in cream sauce. (I suspect the French influence in Beirut initiated the cream sauce anyway.)

Stuffed specialties extend from Artichokes to Zucchini in Middle Eastern cookery. This chapter concentrates on the notable eggplant, grapeleaf, cabbage, and *koosa*. (A light green variety of squash covered with a slight bit of fuzz much like peach skin, *koosa* grows on a vine, rather than in a dense bush like its nearest equivalent, the zucchini.) Expanding on these recipes, you may want to have fun experimenting with herbs or spices, using the general technique for stuffing and saucing.

Initially I was overwhelmed, or should I say confused, by the magnitude of stuffed vegetables, so I have tried to give a brief outline here of some basic concepts.

Small zucchini/*koosa* or eggplants are often reamed out and stuffed whole. Large eggplants are sectioned out, fried, then slit and stuffed. Leaves, of course, are stuffed and rolled. All stuffed vegetables use one of two fillings:

I. RAW MEAT AND RICE FILLING

With tomato in stuffing and with tomato sauce

Grapeleaves
Cabbage leaves
Dried eggplant skins
Fresh eggplant or zucchini (can use rice stuffing with *no* tomato)
Pickled *koosa* or zucchini (can use rice stuffing with *no* tomato)

With no tomato in stuffing or sauce

***Koosa* when *yoghurt* sauce is used**
Cabbage when spearmint and garlic are used

II. COOKED MEAT – PINE NUT STUFFING *(which can include onion)*

This is stuffed into hollowed-out vegetables which are then sautéed and cooked in a sauce, or stuffed into slits of the vegetable which has been fried before stuffing.

Eggplant
***Koosa* or zucchini**

With this method, one of three sauces is used.

Tomato (with or without garlic)
Yoghurt (with or without garlic)
White sauce (may be gratinéed)

Simple, right? Keep this in mind as you read through this section. If a rule of thumb could be made, it might go like this: Take a raw vegetable, stuff it with a raw filling, and simmer it; take a sautéed vegetable, stuff it with a cooked filling, and bake it.

Then you go out, buy a glove with five thumbs, and make up four more rules to include all the variations.

• HOT STUFFED GRAPELEAVES •

MAHSHI WARAK AREESH

Sitti's pride and joy. Ruth says that the butter included in the recipe here is really optional, and that sometimes 1 tablespoon is put on the top of the pot of leaves right before serving to make the rolls look shiny.

Often *koosa* and grapeleaves are stuffed and cooked in the same pot. Spare grapeleaves are poked into the ends of the filled *koosa* to keep in the stuffing. (Zucchini can be used instead of *koosa*.) So, when you are feeling really fancy, ream out cylindrical squash and eggplants, stuff them, and cook along with stuffed grapeleaves. Stuffed green peppers added to the pot enhance both flavor and visual beauty. Particularly patient women have been known to ream out small carrots and onions as well. Imagine the exquisite aromas rising from a platterful of stuffed vegetables of assorted shapes, sizes, and colors. And the beauty.

1 quart pickled grapeleaves (see page 39) *or* **70 − 80 fresh, in season**

BASIC MEAT-RICE STUFFING

1 pound ground lamb or beef
½ cup raw short-grain rice (see Note)
1 t. ground cinnamon
1 t. salt
¼ t. freshly ground pepper
2 − 4 T. butter (see Note)
1 cup drained chopped tomatoes
3 ounces tomato paste (see Note)

BASIC THIN TOMATO SAUCE *(see Note)*

3 cups or more tomato juice *or* **6 ounces tomato paste**
diluted with 3 cups water
¾ t. salt
¼ t. sugar

[8 TO 10 SERVINGS]

WASH the pickled grapeleaves to remove salt brine; or if using fresh, wash and steam briefly to slightly wilt. Remove all stems and drape leaves over the sides of a colander. While grapeleaves dry off a bit, make fill-

sauce. Mix meat, rice, seasonings, butter, tomatoes, and tomato paste together well. (The aunts in the Old Country think we tomato this to death, but we like the aberration.) To make sauce, whisk juice or diluted tomato paste together with salt and sugar until well blended.

As you stuff the grapeleaves, set aside any torn or broken leaves to use as bottom and top layers for the stuffed leaves. To stuff, place one grapeleaf, smooth side down, with stem end facing you. Put 1 large tablespoon filling in the center of the leaf. Roll stem end over filling and fold sides to center, making an envelope. Continue to roll leaf up, toward the tip.

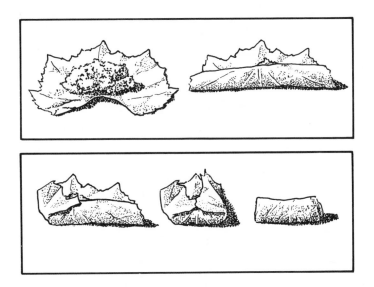

Arrange finished leaves, loose flap down, in tight parallel rows in a 3-quart pot lined with torn or broken leaves. The idea is to keep the stuffed leaves from direct contact with the bottom of the pan. (Browned bones are often put on the bottom of the pan, then torn leaves covering them.) Change direction of each layer by 90 degrees so one layer is north-south, and one east-west.

Cover top layer with more broken leaves. Find a plate of slightly smaller diameter than that of pot and invert to cover grapeleaves; the weight of the plate will help keep the grapeleaves intact and submerged during cooking.

Pour in enough thin tomato sauce to completely cover plate. Bring to simmer, cover pan, and cook slowly for 1½ hours.

Serve hot with lemon wedges or a side dish of yoghurt. The white shawl of yoghurt over the tomatoey-green grapeleaves is lovely indeed!

NOTE: From ½ to 1 cup rice can be used. We prefer using ½ cup. If you do use 1 cup rice, increase tomato paste to 6 ounces and use larger amount of butter. Also increase tomato sauce by 1 to 1½ cups.

• STUFFED CABBAGE LEAVES •

MAHSHI MALFOOF

Among nations, ethnic groups, and families who make stuffed cabbage, there are uncounted versions of this simple delight, which appears to be an all-time, all-class favorite. Even with what we thought was a simple meat-rice-tomato stuffing Middle Eastern – style, we found diversity. Aunt Libby omits all tomato, doubles her rice, and adds garlic and crushed dried spearmint to one version that is very good. Walter's mother, Ruth, uses the basic meat-rice stuffing, but puts it in a whole savoy cabbage, between the leaves – a royal presentation when the cabbage is brought to the table intact!

> **Browned lamb bones (optional)**
> . . .
> 1 recipe basic meat-rice stuffing (see page 153)
> 1 recipe basic thin tomato sauce (see page 153)
> 1 large head green cabbage (3½ pounds or more)
> . . .
> 1 clove garlic (optional – add to pot during cooking)
> Lemon wedges

[6 TO 8 SERVINGS]

IF you have some bones, brown them well in hot oil on all sides and place on bottom of a 3-quart pot. Prepare meat-rice stuffing and tomato sauce.

Remove soiled outer leaves from cabbage. Remove core. Bring 1 quart water to a boil in 4- to 6-quart pan and add cabbage. Cover and "steam" several minutes until outer leaves may be easily removed with tongs. The idea is to wilt the cabbage leaves enough to make them easy to roll. Be careful not to tear the leaves. You will be able to set up a rhythm of removing hot leaves and stuffing cold ones.

Cool wilted leaves a bit and remove large vein, halving leaves along the rib line. Save veins and broken leaves for the base layer in pot. Place a large tablespoon meat-rice stuffing at one end of leaf and roll up like a cigar. As leaves become very small, fill them whole and roll up.

Arrange stuffed leaves over base layer of broken leaves and veins, or browned lamb bones if you have them. Pack snugly, one layer east-west and one north-south, as for grapeleaves. Weight down with plate whose diameter is slightly smaller than the pot's, cover with tomato sauce, and add garlic clove if using. Be sure to remove before serving. Simmer, partially covered, for 1½ to 2 hours.

Serve hot with wedges of lemon, and yoghurt and Arabic bread on the side.

• RUTH'S VERSION •
WITH SAVOY CABBAGE

Pour boiling water over 1 head savoy cabbage, blanching until leaves open. Drain. Stuff with basic meat-rice stuffing, packing stuffing between the leaves. Tie cabbage shut. Submerge cabbage in tomato juice, adding 2 table-spoons fresh lemon juice. Weight down with plate and cook until tender, about 1 hour. Serve cabbage whole and cut it at table.

• LIBBY'S VARIATION •
NO TOMATO, BUT WITH GARLIC AND SPEARMINT

Increase rice to 1 cup in basic stuffing recipe on page 153 and omit tomatoes, tomato paste, and tomato sauce. Stuff cabbage leaves with meat-rice mixture as directed in main recipe. Weight down with plate. Add 2 or 3 cloves crushed garlic, 1 teaspoon salt, and 2 tablespoons crushed dried spearmint to 1 quart boiling water. Pour over cabbage and cook for 1½ to 2 hours. Serve hot with yoghurt.

• STUFFED DRIED EGGPLANT SKINS •

Dried eggplant skins are really interesting. They usually come 12 to a package tied up with string, looking like leathery purple-black wrinkled paper. Sizes vary tremendously, so always buy two dozen in order to have enough "wrappers" for the filling.

12 – 16 dried eggplant skins (see page 6), soaked overnight

.   .   .

1 recipe basic meat-rice stuffing (see page 153)
½ cup finely chopped onion

.   .   .

4 large cloves garlic, crushed
1 recipe (3 cups) basic thin tomato sauce (see page 153)

.   .   .

¼ cup lemon juice

[4 TO 5 SERVINGS]

D RAIN eggplant skins. Prepare basic meat-rice stuffing, using ½ cup rice. Mix stuffing with onion and fill skins to top. Add garlic to tomato sauce and stir to mix.

Set eggplants open end up in pan to fit and pour sauce over them, to cover. Weight down with inverted plate. Cover pan. Bring to boil, reduce heat, and cook slowly a total of 1½ hours. After 1 hour, add lemon juice to pot.

Serve hot with yoghurt and extra juices on the side. Also good sprinkled with crushed dried spearmint.

• STUFFED CYLINDRICAL EGGPLANTS •
IN YOGHURT SAUCE

SHEIKH EL MAHSHI

Like so many little black barques on a sea of white, stemmed cylindrical egg-plants gracefully poke through the yoghurt sauce. To serve, slip a spoon under each eggplant and hold onto the stem while lifting the eggplant from the casserole.

The stuffing here is actually one of the *kibbeh* stuffings. You may wish to vary the filling by substituting other *kibbeh* fillings. As is true in all Mideast cookery, this simple "basic" stuffing lays itself open to all forms of variety: sometimes slivered or chopped onion is added; more pine nuts, or less; more or less cinnamon; the grind of meat ranges from very coarse to fine, and so forth.

If you cannot find cylindrical eggplants, use the variation recipe, which calls for large round eggplants.

8 – 12 (2 – 2¼ pounds) cylindrical eggplants, 4 – 5½ inches long
½ cup vegetable oil for frying

.   .   .

BASIC COOKED MEAT STUFFING

¼ cup pine nuts
2 – 3 T. butter or oil

.   .   .

½ cup onion, chopped or slivered in thin crescents (optional)
½ pound ground lamb or beef, coarsely ground if possible

.   .   .

½ t. salt
Freshly ground pepper (see Note)
½ t. ground cinnamon

.   .   .

3 cups basic cooked yoghurt sauce (see Note)

[6 SERVINGS]

WASH eggplants. Peel in striped fashion lengthwise, leaving stems on. Skin strips will help eggplant to stay together and add visual beauty to the dish. Heat half the oil in a skillet and fry half the eggplants on all sides until medium-dark brown and tender. Repeat with remaining oil and egg-plants. Drain eggplants on paper towels laid over newspapers.

To make basic cooked meat stuffing: Fry pine nuts in butter or oil over moderate heat until medium brown all over, 5 to 7 minutes. Shake pan and stir frequently. Remove pine nuts from pan and set aside. If using onion, add to pan and fry over low heat for 5 to 10 minutes, until onion is limp and browned around the edges. Then add meat and fry over moderate heat another 5 to 7 minutes, until meat loses pink color. Chop up meat well as it cooks. Spoon off excess fat. Sprinkle with salt, pepper, and cinnamon. Return pine nuts to meat mixture; stir well to mix with meat and fry 2 to 3 minutes in order to blend flavors.

In separate pot, heat yoghurt sauce and keep warm. Preheat oven to 400°.

Arrange eggplants in roomy casserole or baking dish with all the stems facing in the same direction. Slit eggplants carefully down the center and push pulp aside with a spoon, to make a large pocket. Stuff with meat mixture. Spoon a tablespoon of hot yoghurt sauce over each eggplant. Carefully pour or spoon enough sauce around eggplants so they are surrounded but not submerged. Place in hot oven and immediately reduce heat to 350°. Bake for 20 to 25 minutes, until sauce bubbles and thickens up and eggplants are well heated.

Serve hot with rice.

NOTE : Freshly ground pepper is hard to measure, but it always tastes better than the already ground variety. If you do measure, ⅛ teaspoon would be suitable for most palates.

Make 3 cups basic cooked yoghurt sauce following directions on page 55 and using the following amounts: 3 cups yoghurt, 1 egg white, 2 teaspoons cornstarch, ¾ teaspoon salt, and a little fresh lemon juice for extra tartness as needed. For this particular recipe, no garlic is specified.

• VARIATION •

Two large round eggplants may be used if you don't have cylindrical ones. In this case, slice off both ends, peel completely, and quarter lengthwise. If unwieldy, cut into eighths. Salt pieces lightly all over and place in a colander for 30 minutes. Pat them dry and fry in hot oil until dark brown. Slit, stuff, and continue as for cylindrical eggplants.

• STUFFED CYLINDRICAL EGGPLANTS •
IN TOMATO SAUCE

SHEIKH EL MAHSHI

Crushed dried spearmint is commonly sprinkled over dishes requiring tomato sauce. The look of rich reds and blacks in combination with a dusting of green is very striking. Prepare *sheikh el mahshi* as on page 157 but use 2 to 3 cups tomato sauce instead of yoghurt sauce.

Walter used to grate half a nutmeg over the meat stuffing, adding the nutmeg at the same time as the cinnamon, salt, and pepper. If you choose to try the nutmeg, use onion in your stuffing and omit the spearmint garnish.

BASIC THICK TOMATO SAUCE

9 ounces tomato paste
2¼ cups water
¾ t. salt
¼ t. sugar

• • •

Crushed dried spearmint

[3 CUPS SAUCE]

WHISK together tomato paste, water, salt, and sugar. Sauce should be very smooth, thoroughly combined. Pour over stuffed eggplants. Bake at 350° for 35 to 40 minutes, until sauce is bubbly. If you want to reduce baking time, heat sauce to boiling before pouring over eggplants and bake only 20 minutes at same temperature. Sprinkle with crushed dried spearmint.

Serve hot on rice with yoghurt on the side.

• STUFFED EGGPLANTS, • GREEN PEPPERS, AND POTATOES, IN TOMATO SAUCE

The stuffed potatoes in this colorful collection of vegetables are most unusual. Who ever heard of stuffing a potato? I've included two cooking methods, one with a thick tomato sauce, and one with a thin; skins are softer on the pepper when you cook this on top of the stove. Sometimes Walter's aunts would fry the eggplants after they were stuffed. Use the pulp from the potatoes and eggplants for making a dip or fritters.

WITH THIN TOMATO SAUCE

4 – 5 cylindrical eggplants (about ¾ pound), 4 – 5 inches long
3 small green peppers (9 – 10 ounces)
3 – 4 small potatoes (9 – 10 ounces)
· · ·
2 recipes basic cooked meat stuffing (see page 158)
· · ·
1 recipe basic thin tomato sauce (see page 153)
1 clove garlic, crushed (optional)

[4 TO 5 SERVINGS]

REMOVE stem and sepals from eggplants. Wash and dry them, then ream them out as you would ream out *koosa* (see page 164), leaving ⅛-inch shell. Cut the tops off the peppers and remove seeds, scraping out large dividing membranes. Rinse them out and drain upside down. Wash and peel potatoes. The flesh of the potato allows for more of a sense of sculpture than the eggplants. Carefully hollow out a cup in the potato, leaving a shell a bit thicker than for the eggplants.

Fill vegetables with cooked meat stuffing. Pack them firmly so stuffing won't fall out during cooking. Place vegetables in a casserole to fit. If the ends of the eggplants are butted up against the side of another vegetable or the pot itself, they may be placed horizontally. Place an inverted plate on top.

Add garlic, if you wish, to thin tomato sauce and pour over, to completely cover plate. Partially cover pan and bring to boil. Reduce heat and cook over low heat for 40 minutes.

Serve hot over rice. Excellent with yoghurt spooned on the vegetables.

WITH THICK TOMATO SAUCE

Often the peppers are steamed 3 to 4 minutes before stuffing to reduce baking time and the potatoes steamed 2 minutes. Baking time would be 45 minutes in this case.

Substitute thick tomato sauce (see page 159) for thin. Do not use garlic with this version. Pour sauce over stuffed vegetables to almost cover. Cover casserole and bake at 350° for 1 hour, or until peppers are tender. Uncover casserole during last 15 minutes to allow sauce to reduce a bit.

Sprinkle with crushed dried spearmint and serve hot on rice, with yoghurt on the side.

• EGGPLANT IN WHITE SAUCE •

BATINJANN BI HALEEB

White sauce never seems typically Lebanese to us, but apparently this is a popular and oft-prepared dish, suspiciously similar to the Turkish moussaka. Perhaps it is the French influence over the years. Tomato and yoghurt sauces are more commonly served; the acidic nature of both complements the richness of the meat and fried vegetables. You may prepare the entire dish a day ahead of time. Baking time will be longer if you do so – about an hour at 350°.

Aunt Helen bakes the assembled eggplant-meat combination in a 350° oven for 10 minutes before she pours on the white sauce. After the white sauce is added, she bakes it another 30 minutes.

3 large round eggplants (about 3 pounds)
1½ cups vegetable oil for frying

. . .

1 double recipe cooked meat stuffing, *without* onion (see page 158)

. . .

1 recipe basic white sauce (see page 56)

[6 TO 8 SERVINGS]

PEEL eggplants. Slice in ½-inch rounds, or halve lengthwise and cut into ½-inch half-moon slices. Salt them lightly on both sides. Place in colander to drain for 30 minutes. Just before frying, pat eggplant slices dry with paper towels.

In a large heavy skillet heat ½-inch oil (to 375° if you have a cooking thermometer handy). Fry eggplant slices 4 or 5 at a time until darkish brown — more than "golden"; the darker color will add richer color and flavor to the finished dish. Drain fried eggplants on absorbent paper.

Have ready the meat stuffing and heat the white sauce. Place half the eggplant in a single layer in large casserole or baking pan (9 by 13 inches or slightly larger). Spread stuffing over eggplants and arrange remaining slices over the meat. Pour hot white sauce over the eggplant.

Bake for 30 minutes at 350°, until nicely browned on top. Dust with paprika for color, if you like. Serve hot.

• *KOOSA* OR SMALL ZUCCHINI • IN WHITE SAUCE

When you halve the squash and stuff their cradles, you end up with a larger pan of stuffed squash, requiring more sauce and feeding more people, than when you ream out and stuff the same amount of squash with the same amount of filling.

6 – 8 *koosa* or zucchini (about 2 pounds), 4 – 5½ inches long
    and 1½ inches wide
3 T. vegetable oil

. . .

1 recipe basic cooked meat stuffing (see page 158)

. . .

1 recipe basic white sauce (see page 56)

[6 TO 8 SERVINGS]

Trim stem ends and nip off blossom ends of squash. Rinse well. Halve lengthwise.

Heat oil. Pat squash dry and fry until slightly browned all over, 5 to 7 minutes. They will be just tender. Place cut side up in a good-sized baking pan (10 by 13 inches or slightly larger).

Have ready the meat stuffing and the white sauce, heated. Scoop out a small cradle the full length of each squash. Save the pulp for dip or fritters. Stuff cradles with meat mixture. Do not sprinkle any extra filling around the squash; you want to keep the sauce white. Spoon a large tablespoon of hot white sauce over each stuffed squash and pour remaining sauce around them. Sauce should not completely cover.

Bake at 350° for 25 to 30 minutes, until sauce is bubbling. Run under broiler for a second or two if you wish to brown the top lightly. This casserole goes well with rice.

· VARIATION ·

To make with sliced *koosa* or zucchini, cut squash in ½-inch rounds. Fry in oil on both sides until well browned. Place half the squash in a layer on bottom of casserole. Spread with meat filling. (You can always make recipes calling for sautéed sliced vegetables with a meat center meatier by doubling the meat filling.) Cover with remaining squash and top with white sauce. Bake at 350° for 25 to 30 minutes.

· *KOOSA* OR ZUCCHINI STUFFED · WITH MEAT IN TOMATO SAUCE

KABLAMA

Squash vary a lot in size, so choose your squash carefully. A good average weight is 4 to 4½ ounces each. Length, 4 to 5½ inches; width, 1 to 1½ inches. You'll need to have a vegetable reamer (see page 4) for this recipe; a paring knife makes a poor substitute.

1 recipe basic cooked meat stuffing, with onion (see page 158)

· · ·

6 — 8 *koosa* or zucchini (about 2 pounds)

· · ·

2 T. vegetable oil

· · ·

2 cups basic thick tomato sauce (see page 159)

· · ·

Crushed dried spearmint

[4 TO 6 SERVINGS]

L ET meat stuffing cool while you prepare the squash. Rinse off squash and cut off the stem end. Nip off the blossom stub as well. Carefully ream out, leaving a shell ⅛ inch thick all around. Be careful not to pierce the bottom.

To ream out squash: Gauge depth to insert reamer by marking spot on reamer with your thumb. Length to penetrate should be ¼ inch less than length of squash. Keep your thumb on that spot to act as a "stopper" as you push in the reamer, and you should have no problems. Rotate reamer around to scrape the sides well. (Save pulp for dip or fritters.)

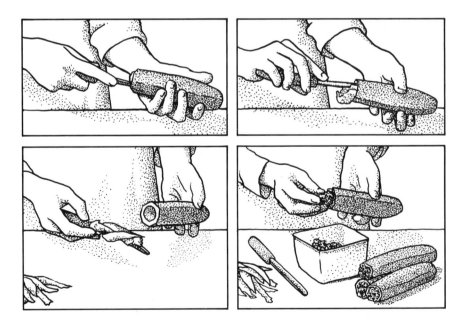

Stuff squash using a spoon and your finger. Thump squash once as you start to fill it; this settles the filling.

Heat oil and fry stuffed squash over moderate heat for 7 to 10 minutes, until they are lightly browned all over and beginning to get tender. Place stuffed squash lengthwise in casserole to fit with enough room for sauce. Pour tomato sauce over them to come three-quarters of the way up. Bake at 350° for 35 to 40 minutes, until sauce is bubbling.

Sprinkle with crushed dried spearmint. Serve with rice and a large dish of cool creamy yoghurt.

· VARIATION ·

This is an expedient preparation with sliced squash that tastes the same but is not as beautiful. Slice squash in ½-inch rounds. Fry rounds briefly in butter or oil until browned. Place layer of sautéed squash in bottom of casserole and top with meat stuffing. Third layer is remaining squash slices. Pour enough tomato sauce over all to barely cover and bake 35 to 40 minutes at 350°.

· STUFFED *KOOSA* OR ZUCCHINI · IN YOGHURT SAUCE I

KOOSA BI LABAN

FOLLOW recipe for eggplants on page 157, substituting 2 to 2½ pounds or 8 to 10 *koosa* or zucchini of the same size as the cylindrical eggplants. Do *not* peel squash. Wash well and remove stems. Fry in 2 to 3 tablespoons hot oil until lightly browned and fairly tender, about 15 minutes. If you prefer your squash *al dente*, fry only 7 to 10 minutes. Slit, stuff, sauce, and bake as in eggplant recipe.

· STUFFED *KOOSA* OR ZUCCHINI · IN YOGHURT SAUCE II

KOOSA MAHSHI BI LABAN

This is a particularly good squash recipe, thanks to Aunt Celia. A tomatoeless meat-rice filling is used in hollowed-out squash, poached first in bouillon, then covered with garlic-yoghurt sauce and baked. You will need a vegetable reamer (see page 4) for this recipe.

> ¾ cup raw short-grain rice
>
> . . .
>
> 9 – 12 *koosa* or zucchini (about 2¼ pounds), 4 – 6 inches long
>
> . . .
>
> 12 ounces ground lamb or beef
> 3 T. butter, softened
> ¾ t. ground cinnamon
> Freshly ground pepper to taste
> ¾ – 1 t. salt
>
> . . .
>
> 1 beef bouillon cube
> 1½ cups boiling water
>
> . . .
>
> 3 cups basic yoghurt sauce with garlic (see page 55)

[6 SERVINGS]

SOAK rice in water to cover for 30 minutes. Wash squash and remove stem end. Ream out, following directions on page 164, leaving a shell ⅛ inch all around. Be careful not to pierce bottom.

Drain rice and save water. Add enough more water to equal 1½ cups and place in saucepan. Set aside. With hands, mix meat well with butter, cinnamon, pepper, salt, and drained rice.

To stuff squash: First make a small slit with a paring knife ½ inch from the bottom end of squash to relieve "back pressure." This will allow you to stuff the squash more easily. Push filling down with forefinger, making sure it goes all the way to the bottom. Squash will give a little near the slit when you press down on filling, if properly filled. Fill each squash to top and place horizontally in a casserole which can simmer on top of the stove. Squash may be stacked two deep, though extra care has to be taken when dishing them up to remove them intact.

Bring reserved 1½ cups water to a boil. Dissolve bouillon cube in water and pour over squash. Cover pan tightly and simmer on top of stove for 20 to 25 minutes, until rice is tender.

Preheat oven to 400°. Heat basic yoghurt sauce.

When rice is tender, most of the liquid should be absorbed. If it is not, uncover pan and cook over moderate heat for 5 minutes or so to reduce the liquid. Pour hot yoghurt sauce over squash and place casserole uncovered in oven. Reduce heat to 350°. Bake 20 minutes, until bubbly.

May be garnished with a light dusting of paprika or crushed dried spearmint.

• STUFFED *KOOSA* OR ZUCCHINI •
IN TOMATO SAUCE

KOOSA MAHSHI

Sometimes one or two stuffed sweet green peppers are cooked along with the squash in tomato sauce. As another variation, squash are often cooked with grapeleaves (see page 153).

[6 SERVINGS]

REAM and stuff squash according to recipe on page 164 and pack squash vertically or horizontally in a large saucepan. You can use rice soaking water to prepare thin tomato sauce (see page 153); pour sauce over squash to cover. Weight down with inverted plate, cover pan, bring to boil, and reduce heat to simmer. Cook for 1 hour.

Serve hot with juices from the pan and yoghurt on the side.

• STUFFED PICKLED *KOOSA* •
OR ZUCCHINI

You may substitute pickled *koosa* for fresh in either of the preceding *koosa mahshi* recipes, or, for that matter, in any of the *koosa* recipes, though I generally stuff them with a raw meat-rice mixture and cook them in thin tomato sauce.

1 quart pickled *koosa* or zucchini (see page 40)

· · ·

½ recipe basic meat-rice stuffing (see page 153), using ¼ cup raw rice

· · ·

2 – 3 cups thin tomato sauce (see page 153)

Soak pickled squash for 8 to 12 hours or overnight, changing water twice. This removes most of the salt in which the squashes were pickled. Drain.

Push meat-rice stuffing into squash using forefinger. Fill to top of squash. Place upright in pan to fit and cover completely with sauce. Weight down with inverted plate. Cover pan and bring to boil. Reduce heat and simmer about an hour. Add more sauce if necessary to keep it covered during cooking. The squash should remain chewy, which makes the dish unique and interesting.

Serve hot with sauce. It is also good with yoghurt spooned over.

• ARTICHOKES IN CASSEROLE, • WITH TOMATO OR WHITE SAUCE

ARDISHAWKI MAHSHI

---

14 – 16 artichoke bottoms or "cups" (two 14-ounce cans)

· · ·

1 recipe cooked meat filling (see page 158)

· · ·

2 cups basic white sauce (see Note)
¼ cup grated Parmesan or Romano cheese

Rinse canned artichoke bottoms in cold water. Drain. Arrange them close together in a casserole to fit. Stuff each artichoke cup with several teaspoons filling. Spread any left over between the cups.

Spoon hot white sauce over and around the cups; you want them poking up through the sauce. Sprinkle with dry grated cheese and bake uncovered for 25 to 30 minutes at 350°. Serve hot.

NOTE: Make white sauce using 3 tablespoons each butter and flour, 2 cups milk, ¼ teaspoon salt, and a shake of white pepper. Follow instructions on page 56.

• VARIATION •

To make with tomato sauce, substitute 2 cups basic thick tomato sauce (see page 159) for white sauce. Bake uncovered for 35 to 40 minutes at 350°. Serve over rice. Good sprinkled with dried crushed spearmint.

• POTATO PIE •

SANEEYEH-T-BATTATTA

Sitti was very proud of this dish and loved to serve it for a company dinner with chicken and rice, *warak areesh* (grapeleaves), *salata* (salad), and sometimes *kibbeh saneeyee* (baked wheat-meat loaf stuffed with pine nuts). She would make the pie in a round pan that had a hole in the center.

> **6 large potatoes (1¾ pounds), peeled**
>
> **. . .**
>
> **3 T. milk**
> **1 large egg, beaten**
> **1¼ t. salt**
> **Large pinch white pepper**
>
> **. . .**
>
> **1¼ – 1½ cups of any of the basic *kibbeh* stuffings (see pages 196 – 197)**
> ** *or* 1 recipe basic meat stuffing (see page 158)**
> **1 – 2 T. butter**
> **¼ cup crushed cracker or bread crumbs (optional)**
>
> [6 SERVINGS]

PEEL potatoes; quarter and slice thin so they will cook through quickly. Steam in tightly covered pan over ½ inch water for 10 to 12 minutes, until tender. Mash potatoes with milk to make them smooth and creamy. You should have about 4 cups mashed potatoes. Beat in egg, salt, and pepper.

Butter an 8-inch ring or round cake mold. If you want to gild the lily, sprinkle crushed crumbs over the mold.

Line mold with half the potato mixture and spread *kibbeh* filling over layer. Spread remaining potato over filling. If you are using crumbs, sprinkle them over the top and dot with butter; or just dot potatoes with butter.

Bake in 350° oven for about 1 hour, until top is well browned. Run a knife around the edges, carefully shake pie loose, and invert onto serving platter.

FISH AND CHICKEN

BAKED FISH WITH LEMON AND GARLIC

Samak bi hamod

176

BAKED FISH WITH *TARATOOR* ON THE SIDE

Samak mishwee

176

DEEP-FRIED PERCH WITH *TARATOOR* SAUCE

Samak maklee

177

FISH BAKED IN *TARATOOR* SAUCE

Tajin

178

FISH WITH WALNUT SAUCE

Samakee harra

179

FISH WITH RICE, ONIONS, AND WALNUTS

Sayyadieh

180

FISH IN WHITE SAUCE

Samak bi haleeb

181

BAKED FISH IN TOMATO SAUCE

Samak bi banadoura

182

CHICKEN AND RICE

Roz bi djaaj

184

MARINATED GRILLED CHICKEN

Shish taouk

185

CHICKEN WITH SUMAC

Djaaj bi summak

186

SPICY CHICKEN AND RICE

Bukhara

187

FISH

FISH fresh from the lake or sea are truly delicious. Recent times, however, have forced us all to consider what we are actually eating, and fish, unfortunately, have been particular victims of our chemical waste. Swimming in the Mediterranean, near Beirut, offshore from the fancy hotels and restaurants, I marveled at the clarity and depth of the azure water...until I encountered a mess of discarded lemons and other questionable garbage floating alongside me. That was thirteen years ago and only what I could see on the surface.

There are also questions in my mind as to the proper way to cook fish. For certain dishes our relatives might first poach the fresh fish 30 minutes, then bake it another 30, really cooking it well done. And, I might add, it tasted very good. Then you have the we-will-cook-it-slowly school, going by the certain-number-of-degrees-done-per-inch method. And finally, included here, there is a slower-bake method at 300° but for a predetermined length of time. I have tried them all over the years spent working on this book. And, though of course everyone says his way is the best, I have concluded the obvious: fish is delicate by nature and should be treated as such.

More specifically, to shallow fry fish, coat it with seasoned flour and cook in hot oil 2 to 4 minutes per side, until golden-dark brown. Keep warm in a 250° oven until all the fish is done.

To deep fry, the optimum temperature of oil is 360°. A thermometer is most helpful. Try not to heat the oil to smoking, for this breaks it down. Remember to fry just a few pieces of flour-coated fish at a time. It cooks more quickly, and without drastically lowering the oil temperature.

To remove the smell of fish from your hands, wash them with vinegar or baking soda.

FISHBONES (1944 – 1970)

When we were kids
during the war
in the summer on sunday
my grandfather, father, uncles
and aunts and cousins would all
converge at the dock in Saginaw,
practically before daylight,
to go fishing, for perch mostly.

Somebody with a rrolling R accent
would have rented the boat (& captain) –
one of those old Great Lake Style
Turn of the Century Square Nosed Prow jobs
with a little window jutting up in the front
to see where you were going, and the sides and back
left all open to the water, on and on to the sky.
In the center was a big ice chest
with the name of some forgotten
soft drink, or beer, nearly rubbed off.

The gunwhales were lined with
greek man-o-war oars of fishing poles,
sometimes you'd catch line & bait
belonging to somebody on the other side
but mostly you'd be pulling in fish
who would spend the rest of the trip
wiggling & flopping in big galvanized wash tubs
brought along from Hamady Hardware, in Flint.

Then before the boat sank from the weight of
our catch, the captain would head for shore
and we'd load up, packing ice on the fish in the trunk –
this was before noon still. (!)

There are famous stories about
Lebanese-Druse drivers, but that is for later,
all I can say is that in the last years

of my grandfather's life, back in the old country,
my grandmother would not ride with him.

As soon as we'd get home
the men would set up an assembly line
in the garage to clean the fish;
one guy'd whack off the head & pass it to
the next guy who'd remove the guts and
somebody would be scaling while
my grandmother prepared the salt & flour
and hot olive oil in the kitchen –

then we would eat.

fresh lake perch deep fried in olive oil,
wrapped in thin pieces of syrian bread
and then dipped in taratoor sauce – (
take sesame seed oil, maybe half cup,
add cold water slowly, stirring to the desired
consistency, a little thinner than you'd like it
because when you add the lemon juice, garlic,
and salt it will congeal a bit –
add a mess of fresh parsley chopped fine
and you're in business.) –

eating was always a monumental joy for us;
the flavors and company deep and satisfying.

Because I was the eldest son of the eldest son, etc.,
the first grandchild & being blessed with 3 young aunts,
my perch, sometimes, was taken off the bones for me,
which meant even more pleasure, in the consumption
as well as in the quantity. I was telling my wife all this

just the other night, we had Red Snapper with Hoisin
sauce, and my wife filleted it for me,
but in spite of her skills there were occasional bones
lingering – I mean, I HATE fishbones (!)
but anybody who believes that fillet stuff is a bit naive;
eating fish is like living life, if you get through it
without hitting any bones, then the fish you ate
never lived, and likely you didn't either.

– Walter Hamady

· BAKED FISH WITH LEMON AND GARLIC ·

SAMAK BI HAMOD

A subtle and delicate flavor . . .

> **1 pound haddock or sole fillets**
> **Several lemons, sliced thin**
>
> **· · ·**
>
> **Several large cloves garlic, sliced thin**
>
> **· · ·**
>
> **½ cup water**
> **3 T. olive oil**
> **¼ cup fresh lemon juice**
>
> **· · ·**
>
> **3 – 4 T. finely chopped parsley**

[3 SERVINGS]

OIL a large baking dish and cover the bottom with half of the lemon slices. Sprinkle garlic over lemon and arrange fish, one layer deep, on top. Spread remaining lemon slices over fish.

In a saucepan, bring water, olive oil, and lemon juice to boil. Pour over fish and bake in 300° to 325° oven for 20 to 25 minutes.

Sprinkle with parsley before serving – with Arabic bread, of course.

· BAKED FISH WITH *TARATOOR* · ON THE SIDE

SAMAK MISHWEE

> **1 pound sole or perch fillets**
> **3 T. olive oil**
> **Paprika**
>
> **· · ·**

TARATOOR WITH PARSLEY

⅓ cup *tahini* (see page 8)
½ – ¾ t. salt
1 large clove garlic, crushed
⅓ cup water
⅓ cup fresh lemon juice
½ cup finely chopped parsley

[3 SERVINGS]

Brush fish fillets lightly with olive oil. Place one layer deep in baking pan and sprinkle with paprika for color. Bake in 300° oven for 30 minutes.

While fish bakes, make the *taratoor*. Measure *tahini* into mixing bowl. Add salt and crushed garlic. Very slowly stir in water. Sauce will get very thick. Still slowly, stir in lemon juice. Sauce will thin out again. Add parsley. Sometimes the parsley is gently mounded on top of the sauce right before serving. If parsley is stirred in, let sauce sit for 15 minutes, then check for consistency. If stiffer than a thick gravy, add a few tablespoons lemon juice. Everyone makes *taratoor* differently, in proportions and consistency, so play around with it.

• DEEP-FRIED PERCH •
WITH *TARATOOR* SAUCE

SAMAK MAKLEE

---

1 pound perch fillets
½ cup flour
½ – ¾ t. salt

   · · ·

Vegetable oil for frying

   · · ·

Lemon wedges
1 recipe *taratoor* with parsley (see page 59)

[3 SERVINGS]

DRY off fish. Combine flour with ½ teaspoon salt and coat fillets well. Heat oil in heavy deep skillet to 360° (see page 11 for advice on deep-fat frying). Deep fry a few fillets at a time until fish are golden brown. Drain them as they finish on a rack or paper and place in 200° to 250° oven until all fillets are fried.

Salt lightly and serve with wedges of lemon, *taratoor* sauce, and Arabic bread.

• FISH BAKED IN *TARATOOR* SAUCE •

TAJIN

Wonderful blend of onion, oil, lemon juice, and *tahini* with the nutty brown flavor of pine nuts amidst the fish!

1 pound haddock or sole fillets

• • •

4 T. butter or olive oil
¼ cup pine nuts

• • •

1 cup onions, chopped or slivered in thin crescents

• • •

½ cup *tahini* (see page 8)
½ cup water
½ – ⅔ cup fresh lemon juice
1 t. salt
1 clove garlic, crushed
Parsley and lemon wedges

[3 TO 4 SERVINGS]

OIL baking dish and break up raw fish into large pieces. Fry pine nuts in butter or oil until evenly brown. Remove and set them aside. Sauté onions in same fat until limp, transparent, and nicely browned around the edges.

Make *taratoor* sauce by placing *tahini* in mixing bowl and slowly adding water, stirring constantly. It will get very thick. Continue stirring, adding lemon juice after water is absorbed. Sauce will thin out again. Use the larger amount of juice if you prefer thin sauces to thicker ones. Blend in salt and garlic.

Add pine nuts and onions to sauce and pour over fish. Bake uncovered at 350° for 40 to 45 minutes, until sauce is thick and bubbly.

Garnish with parsley and lemon wedges and serve with Arabic bread. This is usually served at room temperature, but it is good cold *or* piping hot, eaten as "bites" in bread.

· FISH WITH WALNUT SAUCE ·

SAMAKEE HARRA

Ground walnuts replace the *tahini* of the previous recipe to make a base for this exotic sauce, flavored with garlic and coriander. Cayenne lends heat, which is an unusual element in Lebanese cuisine.

Some cooks prefer to fry the fish before placing it in the sauce to be baked. If you choose to fry it, simply coat the fish with lightly salted flour and fry in 4 to 5 tablespoons hot olive oil, 2 minutes per side. Then prepare the sauce and bake as below.

> **1 pound perch, sole, or haddock fillets**
>
> · · ·
>
> **1½ cups walnuts**
> **½ cup water**
> **½ cup fresh lemon juice**
> **1 t. salt**
> **¼ t. cayenne pepper**
>
> · · ·
>
> **1 small bunch fresh coriander leaves *or* 2 t. ground coriander**
> **6 large cloves garlic, crushed**
> **2 T. butter**
> **Lemon wedges and parsley**
>
> [3 TO 4 SERVINGS]

RINSE or wipe off fish and pat dry. (If fish is frozen, thaw first.) Let it come to room temperature while you prepare the sauce.

Pound walnuts to fine purée in mortar, or use blender. Pour crushed nuts into mixing bowl and slowly add ½ cup water, stirring constantly. Gradually stir in lemon juice and add salt and cayenne. Sauce should be on the thickish side. Pound coriander together with garlic (or finely chop, if you prefer). Fry crushed garlic and coriander in butter until garlic is pale yellow. Add walnut sauce to pan and simmer the whole lot for 10 minutes.

Pour half the sauce into baking dish and arrange fish over it. Cover fish with remaining sauce and bake at 300° for 20 to 25 minutes, until sauce is thick and bubbly. Cool to room temperature before serving.

Garnish with lemon wedges and parsley and serve with Arabic bread.

· FISH WITH RICE, ONIONS, · AND WALNUTS

SAYYADIEH

This dish is especially lovely molded and garnished with fresh parsley and lemon wedges. The dark flavor of the browned onion adds richness and color to the fish and rice.

> **1 pound haddock, cod, or sole fillets**
> **½ cup flour**
> **½ t. salt**
> · · ·
> **4 – 6 T. olive oil**
> · · ·
> **2½ cups onions, slivered in thin crescents**
> **2 cups water**
> **1 cup walnut halves**
> **1 t. salt**
> · · ·
> **1 cup raw long-grain rice**
> **Parsley and lemon slices**

[4 OR MORE SERVINGS]

WIPE off fish and coat with mixture of flour and salt. Set aside to dry for 10 minutes. Heat 2 to 3 tablespoons olive oil in skillet and sauté fish quickly, 2 minutes on a side. Remove to rack or dish.

Add 2 to 3 tablespoons more olive oil to skillet and add onions. Fry *very* dark brown – darker than usual for most stews. Stir in 2 cups water, walnuts, and salt. Simmer 10 minutes, until onions start to dissolve.

Add rice and fish. Bring to boil; reduce heat, cover, and simmer 20 to 25 minutes, until rice is tender. Place fish carefully on bottom of well-oiled mold and pack in rice mixture. Invert immediately onto a large platter and garnish with sliced lemon and parsley.

• FISH IN WHITE SAUCE •

SAMAK BI HALEEB

The white sauce here, from Aunt Alice, calls for an egg as well as some cream, making this much richer than the white sauce found in the sauce chapter. To avoid curdling the egg, be sure to beat the hot sauce slowly and a little at a time into the egg. Do not cook the sauce over direct heat once the egg has been added.

1 pound swordfish or haddock steaks

· · ·

8 ounces fresh mushrooms, sliced
2 T. butter

· · ·

2 T. butter
2 T. flour
½ t. salt
1 cup milk
1 cup cream

· · ·

1 egg, beaten

· · ·

¼ cup grated Romano or Parmesan cheese
Paprika

[3 TO 4 SERVINGS]

PAT fish dry and bring to room temperature. Cut into serving-sized pieces. Sauté mushrooms in 2 tablespoons butter for 10 minutes over moderate heat and set aside.

Make white sauce. In saucepan, melt remaining 2 tablespoons butter over low heat. Add flour and salt and stir well to combine. Cook and stir for 3 to 5 minutes to rid flour of raw taste. Be careful not to brown it. Meanwhile, mix milk and cream together and heat until scalding. Remove from heat and slowly whisk hot milk and cream into flour mixture, beating constantly. Return sauce to low heat and cook until it thickens well, stirring the whole time. Remove pan from heat. In a separate bowl, beat ½ cup hot sauce very slowly into the beaten egg. Slowly stir egg mixture into white sauce and beat until it thickens up.

Pour a layer of sauce into a baking dish. Arrange fish on top and sprinkle mushrooms over fish. Cover with remaining sauce. Sprinkle grated cheese over the top and bake at 350° for 25 to 30 minutes, until bubbly and thick. Garnish with paprika. Parsley always adds some welcome green. Serve hot.

• BAKED FISH IN TOMATO SAUCE •

SAMAK BI BANADOURA

Aunt Helen thinks that this recipe has Moroccan overtones.

> A 1½-pound sole, haddock, or perch *or* 1 pound fillets
> • • •
> 1½ cups finely chopped tomatoes
> 1 small bunch fresh coriander, chopped fine, *or* 2 t. ground coriander
> 6 cloves garlic, crushed
> 3 – 4 T. olive oil
> 3 – 4 T. fresh lemon juice
> 1 T. ground cumin
> 1 t. salt
> ¼ t. cayenne pepper
> Parsley and lemon wedges

[3 TO 4 SERVINGS]

WIPE off fish. Combine remaining ingredients and pour inside and over whole fish (or under and over fillets) placed in a baking dish. Cover dish tightly with foil. Bake at 300° for 30 minutes.

Cool to room temperature before serving. Garnish with parsley and lemon wedges and serve with Arabic bread.

• VARIATION •

This recipe can be made using cooked tomato sauce, too. Omit olive oil, lemon juice, cumin, and lemon wedges. Fry garlic and coriander in 3 tablespoons butter, until garlic is pale yellow. Add scant teaspoon salt, pinch of cayenne pepper, and 2 cups stewed tomatoes or finely chopped fresh tomatoes. Simmer 20 minutes, until sauce thickens. Pour sauce under and over raw fish. Cover baking dish with foil and bake 20 to 25 minutes at 300°.

Serve hot or cold; sprinkle 2 to 3 tablespoons parsley over right before serving. Goes well with plain rice and/or Arabic bread.

CHICKEN

THE scarcity of chicken recipes in this book is inexplicable; what needs to be said is that the few offered are well-loved stand-bys that are served often and always enjoyed thoroughly.

A steaming pot of chicken and rice – dredged with cinnamon and cooked with browned pine nuts and chicken broth, then served with tangy cold homemade yoghurt – never fails to interest one of cookery's most critical audiences – children! For those whose palates ask for spiciness, there is *Bukhara*, chicken heavy with pepper, cardamom, cinnamon, and tomato. *Shish taouk* is a wonderful item for summer cookouts. Deboned chicken is marinated overnight, then skewered along with onions and peppers and served with a very powerful but delicious garlic sauce. In the *fattee* section, try the chicken version, a layered "production" piece which proves itself as tasty as it looks.

· CHICKEN AND RICE ·

ROZ BI DJAAJ

An all-time favorite: very simple and quick, especially if you have your chicken boned ahead of time. Aunt Celia adds 1 teaspoon saffron to the rice as it cooks.

> **A 4 – 5 pound stewing or roasting chicken**
> **2½ – 4 cups water**
> **1 t. salt**
>
> · · ·
>
> **⅓ cup pine nuts**
> **¼ cup butter**
>
> · · ·
>
> **4 chicken gizzards, minced**
> **4 chicken hearts, minced**
> **1 t. ground cinnamon**
>
> · · ·
>
> **3 T. butter**
> **¼ cup raw long-grain rice**
> **1 t. salt**
> **2 cups broth from above**
>
> · · ·
>
> **10 whole almonds (optional)**

[6 SERVINGS]

WIPE off chicken. Cut in large pieces and place in large pot with 2½ cups water and 1 teaspoon salt. (Use 4 cups water if you are thinking of making soup with chicken broth in the near future.) Bring to boil, reduce heat, skim if necessary, and cover pan tightly. Simmer for 1 hour, until chicken is very tender.

Remove chicken from broth. This dish is usually served with skinned and boned chicken, but you may simply cut the chicken into serving pieces if you like it that way. Strain broth and reserve 2 cups for cooking rice.

Fry pine nuts in butter until evenly browned. Remove with slotted spoon. Add gizzards and hearts to fat and fry for 5 to 10 minutes, until well browned. Sprinkle in cinnamon and sauté a few minutes longer. Combine gizzard and heart mixture with all but 1 tablespoon pine nuts and set this mixture aside.

In a 1½- to 2-quart pan, melt 3 tablespoons butter. If you wish to serve the chicken and rice from the pot, use one suitable to place on the table. Sauté rice for 5 minutes. Add 1 teaspoon salt, chicken pieces, heart-gizzard mixture, and reserved chicken broth. Bring to boil. Reduce heat, cover pan, and simmer for 20 to 25 minutes, until liquid is absorbed and rice is tender.

If chicken has not been boned, arrange rice in the center of a large platter and sprinkle with a few optional almonds and the reserved pine nuts. Place chicken in a pattern around rice. The boned version is lovely put in a mold of some kind, if you wish to make your presentation a bit fancier. Oil a 1½-quart mold and place the almonds and reserved pine nuts in a pattern on the bottom. Line with boned chicken and pack rice over the meat. Immediately invert mold onto platter and serve.

Yoghurt is the traditional accompaniment. Any kind of yoghurt salad would also go well with this dish.

· MARINATED GRILLED CHICKEN ·

SHISH TAOUK

---

2 pounds boneless chicken breasts

· · ·

MARINADE I

½ cup olive oil
½ cup fresh lemon juice
1 t. salt
8 peppercorns
¼ t. dried thyme

· · ·

MARINADE II

4 cloves garlic, crushed
Juice of 2 lemons
Thyme, to taste
Paprika or cayenne pepper, to taste
Salt and pepper, to taste
½ cup olive oil

· · ·

2 – 3 sweet green peppers
8 – 12 small whole onions

· · ·

1 recipe garlic sauce (see page 57)

[4 TO 6 SERVINGS]

CUT chicken into 1-inch chunks. Combine marinade ingredients. Marinate chicken for 3 to 4 hours, or overnight.

Wash peppers and cut in large pieces. Peel onions. Alternately thread chicken, peppers, and onions onto *shish kebab* skewers. Grill over charcoal or under broiler in oven. Serve hot with garlic sauce and Arabic bread.

• CHICKEN WITH SUMAC •

DJAAJ BI SUMMAK

Leila sent us this exceedingly easy recipe from Beirut in 1982. The exquisite marriage of sumac, oil, and fat from the chicken skins soaking into the Arabic bread as it bakes makes one wonder how anything so simple can be so complex in flavor and aroma. The flavorful crunchy bread becomes an interesting form of "stuffing."

> 4 loaves Arabic bread
> 1 cup onions, slivered in thin crescents
> Salt and pepper to taste
> 5 T. or more ground sumac (see page 8)
> A 3 – 4 pound chicken, cut in 4 – 6 pieces *or* 2½ pounds mixed legs and
>   breasts
> ¼ cup or more olive oil

[4 SERVINGS]

OPEN up breads so they are one layer thick. Tear them into bite-sized pieces. Line a 10-by-14-inch baking pan with two-thirds of the bread. Spread onions over the bread. Salt and pepper the onions and bread liberally. Sprinkle 2 tablespoons ground sumac over it all.

Place chicken pieces on top of the bread. Generously sprinkle 3 tablespoons or more ground sumac over the chicken. Add more salt and pepper. Drizzle olive oil over the chicken. Cover with remaining bread pieces and drizzle with additional olive oil. Bake at 450° – 500° for 1 hour. Check every 15 minutes as it bakes; if the bread on top begins to get too dark, cover it loosely with foil. Cooking time will depend on the size of the chicken pieces and the oven temperature.

• SPICY CHICKEN AND RICE •

BUKHARA

Thanks to Leila, who has shared some of the spicy recipes her mother, Helen, prepares. The influence of Iran manifests itself in the spice sequence — both its variety and its quantity. Full of flavor yet visually innocuous, the cardamom pods provide an unusual surprise.

2 medium onions, chopped
3 – 6 T. oil
4 carrots, peeled, quartered lengthwise, and sliced

· · ·

1 medium (3 – 4 pound) chicken, cut in 4 – 6 pieces

· · ·

1 cup water
2 medium tomatoes, peeled and chopped *or* 2½ cups stewed tomatoes
1 T. tomato paste
10 whole cardamom pods
1 t. ground cinnamon
1 – 1½ t. salt
1 t. freshly ground black pepper

· · ·

1 cup raw long-grain rice
2 T. ground cumin

· · ·

¼ cup whole almonds
¼ cup pine nuts
1 – 2 T. butter

· · ·

¼ cup raisins

[4 SERVINGS]

SAUTE onions in 3 tablespoons oil until golden. Add carrots and sauté until light brown.

Wipe off chicken pieces and remove any bits of bone. Sauté in pan with onions and carrots, adding more oil if necessary. Brown chicken well. Stir in 1 cup water, tomatoes, tomato paste, cardamom, cinnamon, salt, and pepper. Bring to simmer, cover pan, and cook until chicken is tender, about 25 to 30 minutes. Remove chicken pieces and keep them warm in a slow oven.

Gently stir rice and cumin into sauce. If tomatoes are not especially juicy, you may have to add water. Cover pan and cook over very low heat for 25 minutes, until rice is done. Be sure to check on rice from time to time and give it a stir, as this mixture tends to stick to the pan. While rice cooks, brown almonds and pine nuts in butter over low heat. Remove them and drain off fat.

Serve rice on platter with chicken arranged over the top. Sprinkle with sautéed pine nuts and almonds and the raisins. Any yoghurt salad would go well with this dish, or a side dish of plain yoghurt and some Arabic bread.

LAMB AND BEEF

BAKED *KEFTA* WITH TOMATO SAUCE
Kefta saneeyeh
204

BAKED *KEFTA* WITH *TAHINI* SAUCE
Kefta bi tahini
205

KEFTA LOAF WITH HARD-BOILED EGGS
Kefta saneeyeh bi bayd
206

KEFTA MADE WITH POTATOES, MEAT, AND GARLIC
207

MEAT ROLLS WITH PARSLEY AND PINE NUTS
Filletta
207

MEATBALLS IN TOMATO SAUCE
Daoud basha
209

LAMB IN YOGHURT SAUCE WITH PULLET EGGS
Shemakhleeyee
210

LAMB AND YOGHURT
Laban immo
211

TONGUE WITH CHICK PEAS AND *FARAYKEE* OR *BURGHUL*
Lisanat bi hummous
212

LAMB TRIPE STUFFED WITH CHICK PEAS
Ghammeh
213

BURGHUL OR RICE WITH BEANS AND MEAT
Fasoulia
215

BURGHUL WITH MEAT
Burghul bi lahum
216

· LAMB GRILLED ON SKEWERS ·
(SHISH KEBAB)

LAHUM MISHWEE

The Old Country lamb-raising methods produce meat stronger in flavor, tougher in texture, and leaner than the American counterpart. Commerce is casual: a lamb is brought to the mountain butcher shop, which has a dirt or cement floor with a drain; the lamb is killed and the carcass hung in the open-air shop. Meat is then sectioned off according to the needs of the villagers. For all these reasons people there like to cook lamb until it is well done and bloodless.

Ruth says lamb shoulder was the favorite for grilling because there was always enough fat to keep the *shish* moist. If you decide to use beef: sirloin, T-bone, or other high-quality steaks work very well.

> 4 – 5 pound leg of lamb *or* 2½ pounds boned lamb shoulder (see Note)
> 2 – 3 large sweet green peppers, cut in large bite-sized pieces
> 1 sweet red pepper, cut in bite-sized pieces
> 2 large onions, quartered and separated into layers
>
> · · ·
>
> 4 Arabic breads
> Salt and freshly ground pepper to taste
> Juice of 2 lemons

[6 OR MORE SERVINGS]

REMOVE all gristle, fasciæ, and excess fat from meat, leaving only enough fat on to "baste" meat. Cut into bite-sized pieces. Alternately thread meat, peppers, and onions onto skewers.

Grill over charcoal. We find lamb best when grilled medium-rare (10 to 15 minutes). Walter likes to put green fruit wood or green hickory on top of the charcoal fire. He recommends frequent basting with lemon juice; garlic and lemon juice; or garlic and wine vinegar. If you prefer, *shish kebab* may be broiled in oven until done to your satisfaction.

Use Arabic bread to remove the meat from the skewers onto the plates, giving each person some bread used for this purpose. The bread absorbs the juices from the meat and enhances the flavor of the bite you make of bread, meat, onion and pepper.

Season to taste with salt, freshly ground pepper, and liberal squeezes of fresh lemon juice. Serve *taratoor* sauce (see page 59) as an accompaniment.

NOTE: A 5-pound leg yields about 2½ pounds meat. Save the bone for soup.

· GROUND MEAT WITH ONION, · BURGHUL, AND SPICES

KIBBEH

Kibbeh, the national dish of Lebanon, has a versatility that allows it to assume many shapes with many sauces. It is eaten raw, cooked, baked, sauced, and stuffed. In the Old Country the ratio of wheat to meat is 1:1. Ruth uses a 2:3 ratio, and the meat-eater Druse-mutation Walter Hamady started out with a 1:3, now reduced to a compromise 1:2⅓. There are so many variations to this basic dish that it depends on your taste for spices and meat and wheat. Here's one recipe for the traditionalists, and one of our own adaptations.

In Lebanon, the meat is pounded in a mortar until pasty; the soaked *burghul* is worked well by hand to soften it and then mixed with the meat; the two are then well pounded to make a thick paste. I don't think any of the relatives still do it this way; blenders and grinders are easier, if not so romantic!

TRADITIONAL PROPORTIONS	REVISED EDITION
(from Aunt Libby)	*(USA)*
About 13 ounces lean lamb or beef	20 ounces lean lamb or beef
1 cup fine *burghul* (see page 6)	1 cup fine burghul (see page 6)
· · ·	· · ·
½ cup ground onions plus juice	1½ cups ground onions plus juice
¼ t. ground cinnamon	¾ t. ground cinnamon
⅛ t. ground allspice	½ t. ground allspice
1 t. ground cumin	1 T. or more ground cumin
1 t. or more salt	2 t. salt
¼ t. freshly ground pepper	⅓ t. freshly ground pepper
[3½ CUPS KIBBEH; 16 TO 21 KIBBEH BALLS; 6 TO 7 SERVINGS]	[MORE THAN 5 CUPS KIBBEH; 24 TO 30 KIBBEH BALLS; 8 TO 10 SERVINGS]

Be sure to remove all fat and gristle from meat. Grind meat twice through fine blade of meat grinder. Measure; you should have 1½ cups or 2⅓ cups ground meat, depending on recipe used. Wash *burghul* in a sieve and squeeze out water. Rub well with hands to make it soft. Mix *burghul* with meat and onion. Put mixture through fine blade of grinder twice. Add seasonings and work well into meat with hands until mixture is very pasty and doughy.

If cumin is not freshly ground, use more to taste. Walter likes it strongly cumin flavored, but the relatives think it's too spicy this way. Suit yourself. Ruth says she uses 1 cup *burghul* to 1 pound sirloin tip or round steak, plus a 2-inch diameter onion (⅔ cup grated), more cinnamon, and less allspice. So there you have it.

• RAW *KIBBEH* •

KIBBEH NAYEE

This could be called steak tartar Middle Eastern style. It is eaten as an appetizer, or as main course for those who really enjoy it a lot.

Traditionally a design is pressed into the meat, using a fork or dull knife. Place a mound of *kibbeh* in a shallow dish and draw grooves across the mound in a star shape with a fork, passing through the center point with each stroke. Make a slight indentation in the center of the mound and trickle olive oil over the *kibbeh*. Decorate with finely chopped parsley, bits of chopped scallion, or segments of a quartered white onion separated into single layers. Or form *kibbeh* in balls and score them.

Eat in bites of Arabic bread with small pieces of scallion or onion.

• BAKED *KIBBEH* PATTIES •

KIBBEH KRAS

Form *kibbeh* into small patties, 1½ to 2 inches in diameter and ½ inch thick. Score them with a fork in star pattern. Place on buttered or oiled baking sheet and brush with oil or melted butter. Bake at 350° for 15 to 20 minutes, until golden. Briefly run under broiler for a few seconds on each side, in order to brown them to your liking.

Serve these warm or cold, with Arabic bread and yoghurt.

· BAKED *KIBBEH* WITH LAYER ·
OF PINE NUT FILLING

KIBBEH SANEEYEH

---

1 recipe *kibbeh* (see page 193)
1 recipe any *kibbeh* stuffing (see page 196)
Butter as needed

[10 OR MORE SERVINGS; FREEZES WELL]

HERE again we differ with the traditionalists. Oil a 2-inch-deep pan and pat in *kibbeh* ½ to ⅔ inch thick. The Old Country version insists you make it no thicker than ⅓ inch thick; their thinness combined with the greater amount of wheat to meat produces a crispier, drier *kibbeh* than the one we are accustomed to, so experiment. Sprinkle with *kibbeh* stuffing ¼ inch thick and top with another layer of *kibbeh*, same thickness as first layer.

Score the top with a pattern in diamond or star shapes, occasionally dipping down through both layers with the knife tip. Brush with melted butter

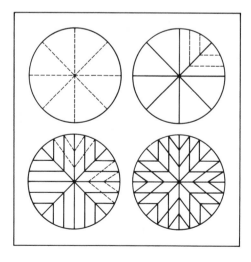

or dot generously with bits of butter. Bake at 350° for 45 to 60 minutes, until the top begins to brown and the meat is well done. Put under the broiler for a few seconds if top is not brown enough. Serve warm with yoghurt on the side.

• BASIC STUFFINGS FOR *KIBBEH* •

I. MINCED LAMB VERSION

This version of stuffing takes more care than the one following, because attention must be paid to mince the meat finely, discarding excess fat and all gristle. The overall texture is more cohesive than the ground-meat variety, and the taste is somewhat richer and fuller.

> 6 T. pine nuts
> 2 – 3 T. butter
>
> . . .
>
> 1 T. butter
> 1 cup minced onions
>
> . . .
>
> 8 ounces minced lean lamb or beef
>
> . . .
>
> 1 t. ground cinnamon
> ¾ t. salt
> ¼ t. freshly ground pepper
> 1 cup water

[1¾ CUPS]

FRY pine nuts in butter over medium heat until nicely browned. Remove with slotted spoon and set aside. Add 1 more tablespoon butter and fry onions for 10 to 15 minutes, until they are light brown all over.

Stir in meat and brown with onions for another 10 minutes. Sprinkle with cinnamon, salt, and pepper. Return pine nuts to mixture. Stir in 1 cup water, cover, and simmer over low heat for 1 hour, stirring frequently. Add more water if it begins to stick to pan. Mixture should be very thick.

II. QUICK GROUND LAMB VERSION

4 T. pine nuts
2 – 3 T. butter
   •   •   •

½ onion, chopped fine (optional)
8 ounces ground lamb (coarsely ground if possible)
   •   •   •

½ t. ground cinnamon
½ t. salt
Freshly ground pepper to taste

[1½ CUPS]

PREPARE as for version I, with or without onion, except that after return of pine nuts to pan, all ingredients should be simmered for only 10 to 15 minutes.

III. MEATLESS VERSION

4 T. butter or oil
¾ cup pine nuts
   •   •   •

2½ cups onions, slivered in thin crescents
   •   •   •

¾ t. salt
1 t. ground cinnamon
Freshly ground pepper to taste

[1¾ CUPS]

MELT butter or oil and fry pine nuts carefully over moderate heat until evenly browned. Remove pine nuts with slotted spoon and set aside. Add onions and sauté 10 to 12 minutes, uncovered, stirring frequently, until limp and light brown all over. Return pine nuts to onions and add salt, cinnamon, and pepper. Cook over low heat another 2 to 3 minutes to blend flavors.

· *KIBBEH* BALLS IN *TAHINI* SAUCE ·

KIBBEH ARNABIEH

Here is a marriage of two favorites of Arabic cuisine — *kibbeh* and *taratoor* sauce. Stuffed *kibbeh* balls are simmered in a thickened *tahini* sauce augmented by browned onions. The subtle piquant flavor of the sauce is a pleasing surprise to the uninitiated. Ruth says to use some cider vinegar if not enough lemon is available.

½ recipe *kibbeh* (see page 193)
¾ cup any *kibbeh* stuffing (see page 196)

· · ·

¼ cup olive oil
2 cups finely chopped onions
1 quart water

· · ·

1 cup *tahini* (see page 8)
1 cup fresh lemon juice

· · ·

3 T. cornstarch
¼ cup cold water

· · ·

1 – 2 t. salt

[5 TO 6 SERVINGS, 2 KIBBEH PER PERSON]

DIVIDE *kibbeh* into 10 or 12 sections and form into tapered footballs. Poke forefinger down center of each and twirl around finger to widen opening uniformly. Stuff each *kibbeh* with 1 tablespoon filling and pinch closed. Reshape into football and set aside until sauce is ready.

In a 2- to 3-quart saucepan, heat olive oil and brown onions for 10 to 15 minutes, until they are soft and tan. Then slowly stir in 1 quart water. Bring to boil and reduce heat to simmer.

Combine *tahini* with lemon juice in mixing bowl by slowly stirring juice into *tahini* in a steady thin stream. Beat *tahini* mixture into onion sauce and simmer several minutes. Dissolve cornstarch in ¼ cup cold water and beat this into sauce. Cook 10 minutes, until sauce thickens. Add salt to taste.

Drop *kibbeh* one at a time into sauce, making sure they are completely submerged. Cover pan and simmer for 30 to 45 minutes.

Serve hot over rice.

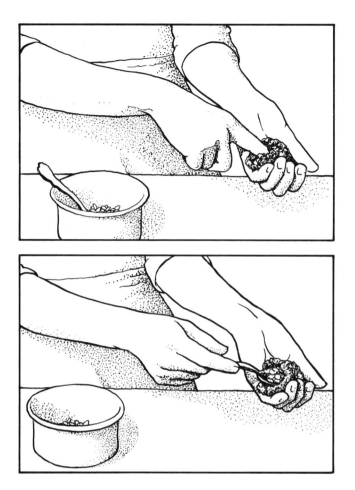

• *KIBBEH* IN YOGHURT-RICE SAUCE •

KIBBEH LABNEEYEE

Definitely one of the most delicious forms of *kibbeh*. Essentially you are dropping *kibbeh* stuffed with browned pine nuts into the yoghurt – lamb broth – rice soup called *labneeyee*, letting them cook in the thick soup, flavors intermingling.

½ recipe *kibbeh* (see page 193)

.   .   .

½ cup pine nuts
3 – 4 T. butter

.   .   .

1 recipe *labneeyee* (see Note)
Crushed dried spearmint

[6 SERVINGS]

DIVIDE *kibbeh* into 12 sections. Form into tapered footballs. Fry pine nuts until lightly browned in butter and stuff each *kibbeh* with 2 teaspoons pine nuts. Pinch ends shut and re-form into footballs.

NOTE: Prepare *labneeyee* as on page 104 with these changes. Use 3½ cups water to prepare lamb broth. Add yoghurt-cornstarch mixture *at same time* as raw rice. Stirring constantly, bring to slow boil. Then reduce heat and cook 10 minutes.

Gently drop *kibbeh* into prepared *labneeyee*, covering them well with sauce. Cover pan and cook slowly for about 20 minutes. Rice will be fully expanded, sauce thick and creamy, and *kibbeh* cooked through.

Serve in soup bowls, sprinkled with crushed dried spearmint.

• *KIBBEH* BALLS STUFFED WITH • WALNUTS AND BUTTER IN *KISHIK* SAUCE

KIBBEH BI KISHIK

Sitti's friend and housekeeper/helper prepared this for us one evening in Baakline, up in the mountains. In his journal, Walter wrote: "I remember her very long thick braid to her waist and below – salt and pepper hair, sturdy braid, like the woman and her knowing-with-love look, penetrating eyes."

We watched her form the *kibbeh* balls, stuffing them with walnuts, and marveled at the sweet smell of cinnamon mingling with the pungent allspice as the *dehen* simmered on the stove. She took the *kishik* powder, a floury wheat and yoghurt mixture, and added it to the spicy lamb-fat *dehen*, thinned it out with water, and cooked it up like a thin version of an exotic porridge.

Once the sauce was ready she dropped the meatballs in and simmered the whole lot together. It was a memorable evening.

This is a hearty mountain form of *kibbeh*, served soup style. It can be a first course or stand as a simple complete meal in itself. For variation, stuff *kibbeh* with mixture of ¾ cup mashed potato and 4½ tablespoons melted *dehen*, or use a basic meat – pine nut filling for *kibbeh*.

> ½ recipe *kibbeh* (see page 193)
> ·   ·   ·
> ¾ cup walnuts
> 3 T. butter
> ·   ·   ·
> ⅓ cup *dehen* (see page 9)
> ¾ cup chopped onion
> ·   ·   ·
> 1¼ cups *kishik* (see page 6)
> 5 cups water
> ⅛ t. ground allspice
> ⅛ t. ground cinnamon
> ⅛ t. freshly ground pepper
> 1 t. salt

[5 TO 6 SERVINGS, 2 KIBBEH PER PERSON; FREEZES WELL]

DIVIDE *kibbeh* into 10 or 12 sections. Crush walnuts with a mortar or rolling pin and mash in butter to form a nut paste. Shape *kibbeh* into tapered footballs, poke a hole in center with forefinger, and twirl ball around finger to widen opening. Stuff with 1 tablespoon walnut filling; pinch end shut and reshape into football. Refrigerate *kibbeh* until sauce is ready.

In a 2- to 3-quart saucepan, melt *dehen* and brown chopped onion until translucent and light brown around edges. Sprinkle in *kishik* and stir well. The *kishik* will absorb the *dehen*. Brown mixture slightly but don't let it burn. Slowly stir in 5 cups water and blend until sauce is smooth. Add spices and simmer 20 to 30 minutes, until it is bubbly and thick.

Slowly drop in *kibbeh*, one at a time. Be sure each is completely covered with sauce. Cover pan and simmer 30 minutes or longer. Sauce will thicken up even more and be like a thick, grainy gravy. Thin with water if unreasonably thick.

Serve hot in soup bowls, 1 or 2 *kibbeh* balls per person, depending on whether it is a soup or full-meal course.

• MEATBALLS WITH PARSLEY AND ONION •

KEFTA

Kefta is the versatile basic meatball of the Middle East. Unlike *kibbeh, kefta* has no grain extender such as *burghul*; instead, a generous amount of parsley and onion add color, texture, and flavor. Cooking techniques for *kefta*, however, parallel those for *kibbeh*. The meat base can be broiled or baked plain; or it can be stuffed with pine nuts and baked in a variety of sauces, such as tomato or *tahini*, to which an assortment of vegetables, including tomatoes, green peppers, and potatoes, is often added.

One recipe calls for wrapping the *kefta*, jellyroll style, around hard-boiled eggs, to form a simple whole meatloaf. Another recipe deletes parsley and onion completely, using potato and garlic instead. Rest assured that there are as many recipes for this dish (and all the others) as there are cooks in Lebanon.

> 1 pound finely ground lamb or lean beef
> 1 cup minced or grated onion
> 1 cup minced parsley
> 1 t. ground cinnamon
> ¼ t. freshly ground pepper
> 1 t. salt

[4 SERVINGS]

Mix ingredients together well with hands, kneading until mixture becomes cohesive. May be chilled an hour or so to make handling easier. Form into tapered footballs and prepare according to one of the following recipes.

· BROILED *KEFTA* ·

KEFTA MISHWEE

DIVIDE basic *kefta* into 8 to 10 balls. Thread each ball onto a *shish kebab* skewer and mold into a thick finger of meat about 4 inches long and no thicker than 1 inch. Broil over charcoal or grill under broiler in oven until meat is well done. Or form into 3- to 4-inch tapered footballs and grill on top of charcoal.

Serve with Arabic bread and *taratoor* sauce (see page 59). Or try this sumac mixture: Sprinkle 1 to 2 tablespoons ground sumac (see page 8) over ¼ cup minced parsley mixed with 1 small onion slivered in thin crescents. Spoon over grilled *kefta*.

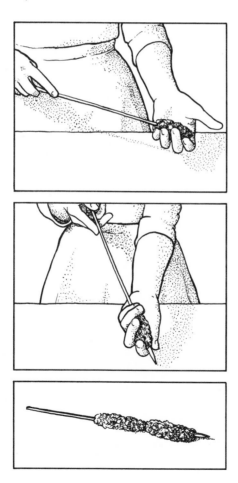

• BAKED *KEFTA* WITH TOMATO SAUCE •

KEFTA SANEEYEH

Kefta is formed into patties or tapered footballs for baking. As in the *tahini* recipe following, the *kefta* may be browned first in the oven before adding the sauce. Some believe this eliminates a "boiled" flavor. Both methods are delicious.

> 1 recipe *kefta* (see page 202)
>
> · · ·
>
> ½ cup pine nuts
> 2 T. butter
>
> · · ·
>
> 6 ounces tomato paste
> ¼ t. sugar
> ½ t. salt
> 1½ cups water
>
> · · ·
>
> 1 t. crushed dried spearmint

[4 SERVINGS]

FORM 8 tapered footballs from *kefta*. Brown pine nuts in butter and use this as stuffing. Poke hole in *kefta* balls and twirl around forefinger to widen gap. Stuff *kefta* with pine nuts and pinch shut. Reshape into football and place in 2-inch-deep casserole.

If you decide to brown the *kefta*, place casserole in a 375° – 400° oven for 15 to 20 minutes. Drain off fat. Reduce heat to 350°.

Blend tomato paste well with sugar, salt, and water to form a smooth sauce. Stir in spearmint now if you wish; or wait to sprinkle it over the baked *kefta*. Pour sauce over *kefta*. Sauce should almost cover. Bake uncovered at 350°: raw *kefta* for 40 to 45 minutes; browned *kefta* for 30 minutes.

Serve hot over rice.

· BAKED *KEFTA* WITH *TAHINI* SAUCE ·

KEFTA BI TAHINI

---

1 recipe *kefta* (see page 202)

· · ·

2 potatoes, peeled and quartered
2 large onions, slivered in thin crescents

· · ·

⅔ cup *tahini* (see page 6)
1 clove garlic, crushed
1 scant t. salt
1 cup water
1 cup fresh lemon juice

[4 SERVINGS]

FORM 8 tapered footballs from *kefta*. Steam prepared potatoes for 5 minutes. Grease baking dish and in it arrange *kefta*, onions, and potatoes. Brown for 20 minutes in 375° – 400° oven, turning *kefta* once.

While *kefta* bakes, make *tahini* sauce. Measure *tahini* into mixing bowl. Crush garlic. Mix garlic and salt with *tahini*. Slowly stir water into *tahini*. It will become pasty and white, then thinner. Add lemon juice slowly and stir or whisk until smooth.

Pour *tahini* sauce over browned casserole. Bake 20 minutes longer, until sauce is thick and bubbly.

Serve hot, with Arabic bread and olives.

• *KEFTA* LOAF WITH HARD-BOILED EGGS •

KEFTA SANEEYEH BI BAYD

1 recipe *kefta* (see page 202)
3 hard-boiled eggs

· · ·

3 T. vegetable oil

· · ·

1 onion, slivered in thin crescents
1 potato, peeled and quartered
1 large tomato, cut in 4 – 6 pieces
2 cloves garlic

· · ·

1 cup water
1 beef bouillon cube (optional)

[4 SERVINGS]

PAT *kefta* into a rectangle ½ inch thick. It is helpful to do this on a piece of wax paper, which will make forming the roll easier later on. Cut off ends of eggs so they'll fit flush together, and place them end to end in straight line down center of meat. Roll up meat like jellyroll and pack it firmly together.

Heat oil and fry roll until evenly browned on all sides. Place in greased casserole. Arrange vegetables and garlic around meat. Add water (and optional bouillon cube) and bake uncovered at 350° for 1 hour.

Remove meat to warm platter. Mash vegetables, adding water if necessary, to make a thick sauce. Serve hot with sauce spooned over meat.

· *KEFTA* MADE WITH POTATOES, · MEAT, AND GARLIC

1 – 2 large cloves garlic, crushed
1 t. salt
¼ t. freshly ground pepper
¼ t. ground allspice

· · ·

½ cup mashed potato

· · ·

1 pound ground lamb or lean beef

[4 SERVINGS]

STIR garlic, salt, pepper, and allspice into mashed potato. With hands, work potato mixture well with meat and form in 8 tapered footballs or in patties. Cook in one of the following ways. Either grill under broiler, turning once to brown both sides evenly; *or* dip in 2 tablespoons flour and brown in butter, frying slowly on both sides until nicely browned and well done.

· VARIATION ·

Sliver a green pepper and an onion, and slice a large tomato. Mound green pepper and onion on top of floured and briefly browned *kefta* patties. Top with tomato slices. Bake at 350° for 35 to 40 minutes until vegetables are tender.

· MEAT ROLLS WITH PARSLEY · AND PINE NUTS

FILLETTA

In Lebanon a bit of the fat from the heavy lamb tail, plus parsley and browned pine nuts, is rolled up in a thin piece of meat. The rolls are browned and then baked slowly with potatoes until tender. As the fat melts it bastes the meat and adds a special flavor to the dish. Since we have to forgo the special brand of lamb fat, try a teaspoon of *dehen* (see page 9) as the viable alternative, or simply use butter.

> **2 pounds round steak**
>
> •   •   •
>
> **⅓ cup pine nuts**
> **3 − 4 T. butter**
>
> •   •   •
>
> **⅓ cup minced parsley**
> **⅓ cup *dehen* or butter**
>
> •   •   •
>
> **Salt and freshly ground pepper to taste**
>
> •   •   •
>
> **4 − 6 T. vegetable oil**
>
> •   •   •
>
> **1½ − 2 cups water**
> **1 beef bouillon cube (optional)**
> **4 potatoes, peeled and quartered**
>
> [6 SERVINGS]

REMOVE all fat from the meat and pound it flat, ¼ inch thick, with the side of a heavy cleaver. (Or ask your butcher for rouladen.) Cut into 3-by-5-inch pieces. Two pounds of meat ought to make 12 to 14 pieces.

Brown pine nuts evenly golden brown in butter. Lightly salt and pepper each piece of meat. Place 1 teaspoon each of parsley, pine nuts, and either *dehen* or butter in the center of each rectangle of meat, and roll up like a cigar. Secure meat rolls with string or short toothpicks. Heat oil and brown rolls well all over.

Place in casserole with water and cover pan. Dissolve bouillon in water for more flavor. Bake at 350° for 1 hour. At the end of 1 hour add potatoes. Cover and bake until tender, about 1 hour. Remove strings and arrange rolls on platter, surrounded by potatoes. Serve hot with juice spooned over the meat.

• MEATBALLS IN TOMATO SAUCE •

DAOUD BASHA

This simple meatball stew is best made with lamb. If you use beef, definitely include the cinnamon. The pine nut stuffing is a delightful surprise in what appears to be a very humble dish. Sometimes the balls are not stuffed. Instead, the browned pine nuts are sprinkled over the simmering meatballs. But, if you have the time, hide the pine nuts inside.

> ½ cup pine nuts
> 3 – 4 T. butter
>
>   .   .   .
>
> 3 cups onions, slivered in crescents
>
>   .   .   .
>
> 1 pound ground lamb or lean beef
> 1 t. salt
> ¼ t. freshly ground pepper
> 1 t. ground cinnamon (optional)
>
>   .   .   .
>
> ½ cup flour
> 4 T. vegetable oil
>
>   .   .   .
>
> 2½ – 3 cups tomato juice *or* stewed tomatoes
> 2 – 3 T. tomato paste
> ¼ t. sugar
> ½ t. salt
>
>   .   .   .
>
> Chopped parsley *or* crushed dried spearmint

[4 TO 6 SERVINGS]

BROWN pine nuts in butter until evenly golden brown. Remove with a slotted spoon and set aside. Add onions to butter, adding more butter or some oil if necessary, and sauté them until light brown and soft. Remove onions from pan and set aside. Combine meat with salt, pepper, and cinnamon. Form 20 to 24 balls the size of a walnut. Stuff each ball with 1 teaspoon pine nuts and pinch shut. Roll balls in flour and brown well in vegetable oil. Return onions to pan.

Blend tomato juice or tomatoes with paste, sugar, and ½ teaspoon salt. Pour over meatballs. Partially cover pan and simmer for about an hour.

Sprinkle with chopped parsley or crushed dried spearmint and serve hot over rice.

• LAMB IN YOGHURT SAUCE • WITH PULLET EGGS

SHEMAKHLEEYEE

Pullet eggs are poached in a meaty yoghurt sauce, cousin to *laban immo* (see next recipe) and yoghurt soup, and served over rice. A sprinkling of crushed dried spearmint adds lovely color and flavor to the blanket of white. Ruth commented on the eggs: "If the sauce is boiling when the eggs are dropped in, the egg white has a very feathery 'found object' look with streamers and fragments. Sitti cooked her eggs hard-boiled. Philistine Walter likes his poached with soupy rubbery yolks. Ychch!" As you can see, there is much leeway after the eggs are dropped into the sauce. *Shemakhleeyee* is good with *loubieh bzeit* (see page 132). Aunt Frieda was famous for this dish.

1½ cups finely chopped onions
3 T. vegetable oil

. . .

1 pound lamb or beef chunks, shoulder or leg
1 t. ground cinnamon
1 t. salt
¼ t. white pepper
2 cups water

. . .

1 quart yoghurt
½ – 1 t. salt
1 clove garlic, crushed
1 T. cornstarch dissolved in 2 T. water
1 egg or egg white, slightly beaten

. . .

6 pullet or very small eggs

. . .

Crushed dried spearmint

[6 SERVINGS]

IN a large heavy pot, fry onions in oil until medium brown and soft. Remove from pan with slotted spoon. Pat meat chunks dry and brown well on all sides, adding more oil if necessary. Sprinkle meat with cinnamon, salt, and pepper. Return onions to pot, add water, and bring to boil. Reduce heat, cover pan, and simmer for 1 to 1½ hours, until meat is tender.

Stir yoghurt together with ½ to 1 teaspoon salt, garlic, dissolved cornstarch, and egg or egg white. Pour over meat and cook over low heat, stirring constantly until sauce thickens a bit, 5 to 10 minutes.

Carefully break eggs, one at a time, into a saucer. Slip each egg into simmering sauce, guiding eggs with a spoon so they do not touch. Cover pools of egg with sauce and lower heat. Cook for 8 to 15 minutes, depending on how you like your eggs set.

Serve hot over rice and top each serving with an egg. Sprinkle crushed dried spearmint over top.

· LAMB AND YOGHURT ·

LABAN IMMO

The original recipe called for a lamb bone broth with optional meat chunks, similar in preparation to *shemakhleeyee* but without the eggs, and not as unusual.

8 – 10 small whole onions, peeled
3 T. vegetable oil

· · ·

1 pound lamb bones (optional but recommended)
1 pound lamb or beef chunks, shoulder or leg
½ t. ground cinnamon
1 t. salt
¼ t. white pepper
2 cups water

· · ·

1 quart yoghurt
½ – 1 t. salt
1 clove garlic, crushed
1 T. cornstarch dissolved in 2 T. water
1 egg or egg white, slightly beaten

· · ·

¼ cup pine nuts sautéed in 3 T. butter, and chopped parsley;
    or crushed dried spearmint

[6 SERVINGS]

FRY onions in oil until medium to dark brown and set them aside. If you have lamb bones, brown them and cook with the meat, to add more flavor, until meat is well browned. Sprinkle meat with cinnamon, 1 teaspoon salt, and pepper. Add 2 cups water and bring to a boil. Reduce heat, cover pan, and simmer for 1 to 1½ hours, until meat is tender.

Stir yoghurt together with ½ to 1 teaspoon salt, garlic, dissolved cornstarch, and egg or egg white. Pour over meat, add onions, and cook over
low heat for 20 to 30 minutes, until sauce is a well-thickened gravy and
onions are tender.

Serve hot over rice. Garnish each serving with *either* browned pine nuts
and chopped parsley, *or* crushed dried spearmint.

· TONGUE WITH CHICK PEAS ·
AND *FARAYKEE* OR *BURGHUL*

LISANAT BI HUMMOUS

Faraykee becomes very special in combination with chick peas, onions, and
pieces of tongue. The texture and taste are different from *burghul*, so an un-
suspecting guest might have trouble pinpointing the source of the mysterious flavor.

This dish is especially beautiful unmolded on a platter and garnished
with parsley. The meat and onions form patterns on the top.

½ cup dry chick peas, soaked overnight in 1½ cups water

· · ·

1 beef tongue *or* 6 − 7 lamb tongues
3 cups water
1 stick cinnamon
8 peppercorns
1 t. salt
1 bay leaf

· · ·

3 T. butter or vegetable oil
6 − 8 small whole onions, peeled
1 cup onions, slivered in thin crescents
1 cup water or broth

· · ·

2 cups broth from tongue
1 t. salt
¼ t. freshly ground pepper
1 t. ground cinnamon
1½ cups *faraykee* or large *burghul* (see page 6)

· · ·

Lemon wedges
Parsley

[4 TO 6 SERVINGS]

IN a large pan cover tongue with 3 cups water and add seasonings. Cover and cook for 2 to 2½ hours, until tongue is tender. Lamb tongues will take 45 minutes.

While tongue cooks, heat butter or oil and fry whole onions until well browned on all surfaces. Set them aside. Add slivered onions to fat and fry until slightly browned around the edges. Drain chick peas, reserving juice, and stir them into onions. Add enough water or broth to juice to equal 1 cup liquid and stir into chick peas. Simmer 45 to 60 minutes, until very tender. Liquid should be absorbed.

Once tongue is tender, remove from pan, reserving and straining broth. Cool slightly and skin. Remove any fatty tissue and unsightly vessels. Cut tongue in ½-inch slices and place in ovenproof dish. Cover meat with some extra broth and keep warm in a 200° oven until ready to use.

Pour 2 cups reserved tongue broth into tender chick peas. Add whole onions, 1 teaspoon salt, pepper, and ground cinnamon. Heat through. Sprinkle *faraykee* or *burghul* over simmering broth. Cover pan and cook 30 to 40 minutes, until all the liquid is absorbed. If you use *burghul*, reduce cooking time to 25 to 35 minutes. The grain will be tender and fluffy.

Place reserved pieces of tongue on bottom of an oiled mold and arrange whole onions in a pattern with the meat. Pack grain mixture on top of this and invert onto platter. Serve hot with yoghurt on the side. Garnish with lemon wedges and parsley sprigs.

· LAMB TRIPE STUFFED ·
WITH CHICK PEAS

GHAMMEH

(from Aunt Alice)

Tripe at its best is very good. Use veal or lamb tripe for this dish. Pockets are made of tripe, which are then stuffed with rice, meat, onion, spices, and chick peas. After being sewn shut, the pockets are boiled like dumplings, then later cut open and shredded.

½ cup dry chick peas, soaked overnight in 1½ cups water

. . .

1¼ pounds lamb or veal tripe (see Note)

. . .

STUFFING

1 cup raw rice
1 cup chopped onions
1 pound ground lamb
½ t. ground cinnamon
¼ t. freshly ground pepper
1½ t. salt

. . .

3 – 4 quarts water
1 t. salt
¼ t. ground cinnamon

[4 TO 6 SERVINGS]

SKIN and split chick peas as outlined on page 73. Wash tripe and cut into large 6-by-3-inch pieces. Fold rectangles in half and sew 2 sides shut with string. Combine chick peas with rice, onions, lamb, cinnamon, pepper, and ½ teaspoon salt. Fill each tripe bag two-thirds full to allow for expansion during cooking. Sew pocket shut.

Bring 3 to 4 quarts water to a boil and add 1 teaspoon salt plus ¼ teaspoon cinnamon. Drop stuffed tripe in water and return to boil. Skim. Reduce heat to simmer, cover pan, and cook for 1 hour, until chick peas, rice, and meat are well done. Remove bags. Discard string; carefully spoon stuffing onto a large platter.

With a sharp knife, shred tripe into very fine thin strips and arrange over stuffing. Sprinkle with cinnamon, if desired. Serve hot with yoghurt and Arabic bread.

NOTE: You may have trouble locating lamb tripe unless you live in a big city or know a farmer with lambs. Beef tripe does *not* make a suitable substitution.

· *BURGHUL* OR RICE WITH BEANS · AND MEAT

FASOULIA

This could be called a Middle Eastern version of the French cassoulet! The second version, which includes tomato and omits *burghul*, is served with rice; both versions have complementary protein relationships: beans and wheat (grain) and beans with rice.

VERSION I (AUNT LIBBY'S)

½ cup dry northern beans
2 cups water

· · ·

4 ounces salt pork or bacon, cut into slivers
1 pound lamb, beef, or pork, cut into cubes
2 cups onions, slivered in thin crescents

· · ·

3 – 3½ cups water
½ t. ground cinnamon
1½ t. or more salt
¼ t. freshly ground pepper
1 – 2 beef bouillon cubes

· · ·

1 cup large *burghul* (see page 6)
1½ cups water

[6 SERVINGS]

RINSE beans and soak overnight in 2 cups water (see page 72). Fry salt pork or bacon slowly until it releases enough fat to fry meat. Remove and set aside. Brown meat cubes well on all sides, frying a few pieces at a time. Set them aside and add onions to pan, frying until they are light brown. Return salt pork or bacon and meat to pan.

Drain beans (reserving liquid) and add them to meat. Add enough more water to bean water to equal 3½ cups, and stir water, cinnamon, salt, pepper, and bouillon cube(s) into meat and beans.

Cover and simmer for 2 to 2½ hours, until beans are very tender. Sauce should be thick. Add 1½ cups water and sprinkle *burghul* over meat. Cover and simmer an additional 20 to 30 minutes, until wheat is fluffy and tender. If you want a more porridgey consistency, add more water.

Serve hot with Arabic bread, scallions or quartered onion, and a side dish of yoghurt.

VERSION II

Beans and onions are more bountiful in this version, with tomato sauce.

Use the above recipe with these changes. Increase beans to 1 cup dry, soaked in 1 quart water. Increase onions to 3 cups. Increase water from 3½ to 4½ cups. Omit cinnamon, *burghul*, and extra water.

[4 TO 6 SERVINGS]

THEN prepare as above, adding 6 ounces tomato paste plus 1 teaspoon sugar to beans after they have simmered with meat for 2½ hours and become very tender. Simmer 45 to 60 minutes longer, or until sauce really thickens. Add salt and freshly ground pepper to taste.

Serve hot over rice.

• *BURGHUL* WITH MEAT •

BURGHUL BI LAHUM

Consistency may be varied by using either more tomato or less *burghul*. Although allspice is called for here, 1 teaspoon ground cinnamon could be substituted. For a meatless tomato with *burghul*, see page 146.

3 large onions
3 – 4 T. butter
1¼ pounds lamb stew meat

· · ·

1 t. salt
Freshly ground pepper to taste
½ t. ground allspice

· · ·

2½ cups stewed tomato *or* 6 ounces tomato paste
      diluted in 18 ounces water

· · ·

1 cup large *burghul* (see page 6)

[4 SERVINGS]

F RY onions in butter until tender. Add meat to onions and brown well. Stir in salt, pepper, and allspice. Add 1½ cups tomatoes or diluted paste and simmer meat in covered pan for 1 hour. When meat is tender, add another cup tomato mixture and sprinkle *burghul* over meat. Cover and simmer 20 to 30 minutes, until wheat is tender.

Serve hot with Arabic bread, scallions or quartered onion, and lots of freshly ground pepper.

STEWS

STEWS are one of the potentially great one-pot meals. Nothing surpasses the flavors of garden-fresh vegetables. When fresh, quickly browned meat is added, plus cinnamon, salt, and pepper, the basic Lebanese stew is ready either to simmer on top of the stove or to bake in a more leisurely way in the oven.

When Walter and I traveled to Lebanon, we had limited experience with the basic stews. *Saneeyeh bil fern,* an oven stew made with cauliflower, onion, tomato, zucchini, eggplant, green beans, and meat, was familiar to us, but top-of-the-stove stews and the ground-meat-plus-pine-nut variety were unknown; the latter two became welcome additions to our recipe list. Lamb was always used in Lebanon, but Sitti actually preferred using beef once she crossed over to the States.

For the basic stew, some onion is usually browned in vegetable oil; then meat is browned, and liquid, in the form of either water or tomato, is added. Depending on what is in season, vegetables are placed over the meat and then simmered on top of the stove; or layers of lightly browned vegetables are placed with the meat in a casserole and baked for several hours.

Ground meat stew is the basic cooked meat and pine nut combination, with or without onion. Sliced tomatoes and one or two other vegetables, like onions and green beans, are layered over the meat. The whole is then baked and served on rice. The simplicity of this variety of stew and the ease of its preparation make it a good recipe to use when you are pressed for time. For instance, with the simple addition of fresh washed spinach to the simmering meat-nut mixture, you have a nutritious vegetable dish ready to crown a bed of white rice in less than half an hour.

Even though the stews are simple, the method of assembling them varies from person to person. One aunt likes to brown her meat all at once; then she adds the onion to cook right along with the meat. Another fries the meat a few pieces at a time. Ruth cooks the onion first and adds some water; this mixture simmers until a purée of sorts forms. Then the meat is browned separately and combined with the onion sauce. Of course, variation arises concerning placement and combination of vegetables, to say nothing of the shape of the vegetable – whether it should be sliced, slivered, or cubed, etc. One point the Lebanese contingent agreed on, however, was the use of vegetable oil for frying the meat and onion, as opposed to the use of olive oil. They insisted that olive oil should not be used because it would alter the flavor of the stew; the integrity of each vegetable had to be protected through the use of a flavorless oil. (One family in the American-Lebanese group, however, swears by olive oil because the flavor of the oil is so rich and wonderful!) Another tip is to sauté all fresh vegetables quickly in oil before adding them to the stew. With the exception of one stew, which actually incorporates the rice, all forms of stew are to be served on, or accompanied by, rice.

During those months of summer abundance when the garden is bulging with produce, the oven stew proves especially useful. Add what you have a lot of and are hungry for; then enjoy the aromas and your friends while a lovely feast cooks slowly in the oven.

· BASIC STEW WITH GREEN BEANS ·

YAKHNIT LOUBIEH

This recipe gives the essence of Sitti's stews. In all the lamb chunk stews, the method is the same. Variation in vegetables determines the name of the stew.

> 3 T. vegetable oil
> 1 pound fresh green beans, washed and stemmed
>
> · · ·
>
> 1 cup or more onions, chopped or slivered in thin crescents
>
> · · ·
>
> 1 pound lamb shoulder, or beef, cut into chunks
> 1 t. ground cinnamon, or more to taste
> 1 t. salt
> Freshly ground pepper to taste
>
> · · ·
>
> 1 quart canned tomatoes *or* 4 – 6 skinned fresh tomatoes, sliced

[4 TO 6 SERVINGS]

LEAVE beans whole or cut into segments. Then sauté for a few minutes to coat them well with oil. Remove and set aside. Add onions to oil and fry until light brown and limp. Remove.

Trim most of the fat off the meat and cut into bite-sized pieces. Dry meat and brown well in same oil, a few pieces at a time, adding more oil if necessary. Return all meat to pan and sprinkle with cinnamon, salt, and pepper. Spread onions over meat and top with green beans.

Pour canned tomatoes over stew, or arrange fresh tomatoes in a thick layer to cover.

Cover pan and simmer over very low heat until meat is tender, 1¼ to 1½ hours. Stir or shake pan occasionally.

Serve hot over rice.

For the following stews, base preparation on preceding stew with green beans.

· EGGPLANT STEW ·

YAKHNIT BATINJANN

[4 TO 6 SERVINGS]

SUBSTITUTE 1 large (1 pound) round eggplant for green beans. Peel eggplant, if you wish, and cut into ½-inch slices. Divide each round into 4 to 6 wedges. (Or cut the eggplant into 1-inch cubes.) Salt lightly and drain in colander 30 minutes. Pat dry and fry quickly in ½ cup hot oil until lightly browned. Add to stew after meat has simmered 1 hour and is almost tender. Simmer 20 to 25 minutes longer, until tender. You may want to uncover pan during last 15 minutes to allow juices to reduce a bit.

For another eggplant stew recipe, see page 229.

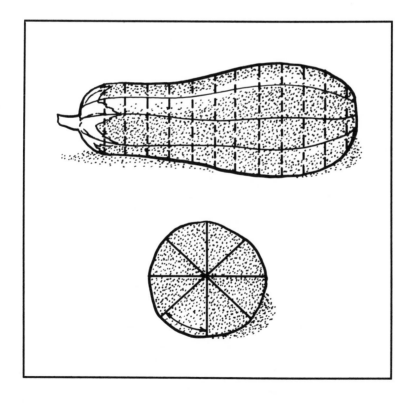

· OKRA STEW ·

BAMIEH BI LAHUM

[4 TO 6 SERVINGS]

SUBSTITUTE 1 pound fresh okra for green beans. Wash and dry off okra. Cut in ½-inch rounds. Fry before adding to stew. These may be added at the same time as the tomatoes. Usually 1 clove crushed garlic is added to okra stews, too.

· *KOOSA* OR ZUCCHINI STEW ·

YAKHNIT KOOSA

[4 TO 6 SERVINGS]

SUBSTITUTE 1 pound *koosa* or zucchini for green beans. Wash squash and cut off ends. Slice in ½-inch rounds. Fry in 2 tablespoons vegetable oil for 7 to 10 minutes, until light brown on both sides. Add to stew after meat is fully tender and simmer 20 minutes longer.

· CAULIFLOWER STEW ·

YAKHNIT QARNABEET

[4 TO 6 SERVINGS]

SUBSTITUTE 1 large head (1½ pounds, untrimmed) cauliflower for green beans. Wash cauliflower. Cut off leaves and remove core. Break into large bite-sized flowerets. Dry off pieces and fry for 10 to 15 minutes in 4 to 5 tablespoons hot oil until medium brown all over. Set aside. Add cauliflower to stew after meat has cooked for 1 hour. Simmer another 20 to 25 minutes. Uncover during last 10 minutes to reduce juices.

• TOMATO AND LAMB STEW WITH EGGS •

BAYD BI BANADOURA

The basic stew changes enormously by simply replacing the major vegetable with eggs. After the meat is tender, eggs are cracked gently into the cooking stew and cooked until set. This dish is good cold for breakfast, as leftovers ...if there are any.

1 cup coarsely chopped onions
3 – 4 T. vegetable oil

· · ·

1 pound lamb, cut into chunks

· · ·

1 t. ground cinnamon
1 t. salt
Freshly ground pepper to taste

· · ·

1 quart canned tomatoes *or* **1½ pounds fresh tomatoes**

· · ·

4 large eggs

[4 TO 5 SERVINGS]

FRY onions in hot oil until limp, translucent, and lightly browned around the edges. Remove from pan. Add lamb chunks a few at a time and brown well. Return onions to lamb and sprinkle with cinnamon, salt, and pepper to taste. Add half the tomatoes plus all the juice to pan. Cover and simmer for 1 hour, until lamb is tender.

With side of spoon, cut up remaining tomatoes and stir them into meat. Gently crack eggs into sauce and stir only enough to break the yolks and prevent them from sticking to pan. Cover pan and simmer over low heat for 10 to 15 minutes, until eggs are set. Eggs should be in small nonhomogenized chunks.

Serve hot with lots of freshly ground pepper and Arabic bread.

• CAULIFLOWER AND *TAHINI* STEW •

YAKHNIT QARNABEET BI TAHINI

Aunt Libby treated us to this delicious stew on her veranda in Beirut in 1972. Her recipe favors using ½ teaspoon cinnamon, but we found we preferred using a whole teaspoon.

> **1 pound lamb or beef, cut into chunks**
> **3 T. oil or shortening**
>
> · · ·
>
> **2 large onions, slivered in thin crescents**
> **¾ cup water**
> **½ – 1 t. ground cinnamon**
> **1 t. salt**
> **Freshly ground pepper to taste**
>
> · · ·
>
> **1 large head cauliflower**
> **4 T. oil**
>
> · · ·
>
> **½ cup *tahini* (see page 8)**
> **½ cup water**
> **½ cup fresh lemon juice**
> **½ t. salt**

[4 TO 6 SERVINGS]

BROWN lamb a few pieces at a time in hot oil. Set aside. Stir in onions and sauté until they are light brown and soft. Add ¾ cup water, cinnamon, 1 teaspoon salt, and pepper. Cover pan and simmer for 1½ hours, until lamb is very tender. Stir occasionally so meat doesn't stick; add more water if necessary.

While meat cooks, prepare cauliflower. Wash and remove core, then break into small, manageable flowerets. Pat dry and fry them in hot oil for 10 to 15 minutes, until light to medium brown all over. (We've also fried them fairly dark brown, which gives the stew a richer, darker flavor.) When meat is tender, place cauliflower on top and simmer for 5 minutes.

Pour *tahini* into a mixing bowl and slowly stir in ½ cup water (see page 59 for more on the texture). Then slowly stir in lemon juice and whisk until smooth. Salt to taste. Pour sauce over stew and simmer, uncovered, for about 10 minutes. Sauce should have a heavy gravy consistency.

Serve hot over rice.

• GREEN BEAN OVEN STEW •

Here is the top-of-the-stove stew, oven style, using fresh beans and tomato. This has more onion and more tomato than the similar *yakhnit loubieh*.

> 1 pound lamb, cut into chunks
> 1 t. ground cinnamon
> 1 t. salt
> Freshly ground pepper to taste
>
>   • • •
>
> 3 – 4 T. vegetable oil
>
>   • • •
>
> 3 large onions, sliced thick
> 6 large tomatoes, sliced thick
> 1 pound fresh green beans
> Salt

[4 SERVINGS]

BROWN lamb chunks: in a large, 3½- to 4-quart casserole, toss lamb chunks with cinnamon, 1 teaspoon salt, and pepper. Pour in vegetable oil and coat meat well. Place uncovered casserole in 450° oven and bake 10 to 15 minutes, stirring meat frequently. Remove casserole from oven. Reduce temperature to 325°.

Cover meat with a layer of sliced onions. Slice half the tomatoes in thick layer over the onions and cover with whole green beans. Top with another layer of tomatoes. Salt lightly. Cover casserole and bake for 2 to 2½ hours. Uncover for last 45 minutes to reduce juices.

Serve hot with rice.

• CLASSIC OVEN STEW •

SANEEYEH BIL FERN

This potpourri of fresh vegetables simmered with lamb until well done is colorful and geared for summer abundance. With a handful of many vegetables, quite a large casserole results, pleasing a group of friends with a minimum of effort. The ingredients are basically the same for this oven stew as for the top-of-the-stove stews, but the method is all oven — longer simmering time and a more diverse arrangement of vegetables.

The shape of your pan is important. The stew won't cook right in a deep vessel. A shallow (4 to 5 inches deep), broad pan works best to evaporate the juices properly; reducing the sauce intensifies the flavor. Like most Lebanese dishes, this is a good leftover.

1 pound lamb or beef shoulder, cut into chunks
2 t. or more ground cinnamon
2 t. salt
¼ t. freshly ground pepper
3 – 4 T. vegetable oil

. . .

1 large eggplant
1 very small cauliflower
6 – 8 small onions
1 pound fresh green beans
2 – 4 zucchini or *koosa*, 4 – 6 inches long
8 ounces fresh okra
6 large fresh tomatoes ⎤
1 cup water ⎦ *or* 1½ quarts stewed tomatoes

[8 TO 10 SERVINGS]

IN a large casserole toss meat with cinnamon, salt, pepper, and oil. Brown uncovered in oven at 450° for 10 to 15 minutes, stirring frequently.

While meat browns, prepare vegetables. Peel eggplant and slice in ½-inch rounds. Cut each round into 4 to 6 wedges. Remove leaves from cauliflower; wash, core, and break into small flowerets. Peel whole onions. Wash and stem beans. Either break in half or leave them whole. Slice washed zucchini or *koosa* into ½-inch rounds. Clean okra and chop into 1-inch pieces.

Now that your work is done, the fun begins! Remove casserole from oven and reduce heat to 300°. Layer vegetables in casserole: beans over meat, then onion, cauliflower, okra, and eggplant. Lightly salt and pepper layers as you build up. Top with sliced fresh tomatoes and add 1 cup water; or pour stewed tomatoes over the vegetables.

Cover pan and bake a total of 2 hours. Uncover during last hour to allow juices to reduce. Meat should be tender and vegetables well done, but certainly not mushy.

Serve hot over rice.

· EGGPLANT, LAMB, AND RICE STEW ·

MAKLOUBI BI BATINJANN

We were told to "invert stew onto a platter and serve." If stew looks stiff enough, run a knife around the edges and carefully turn out onto a platter. It can be done. If you wish to do this, an appropriate pan should be used to cook stew in – a high-sided, deep pot rather than a low flat skillet – just for sheer convenience of unmolding and of course having a platter large enough to "catch" the mold.

> 3 – 4 T. vegetable oil
> 1 pound lamb or beef, cut into chunks
> 1½ t. salt
> ¼ t. freshly ground pepper
> ½ – 1 t. ground cinnamon
> · · ·
> 1 cup water
> · · ·
> 1 large round eggplant
> Salt to taste
> ¾ cup raw rice
> ½ cup vegetable oil
> · · ·
> 5 – 6 cloves garlic
> · · ·
> 2 cups drained canned tomatoes *or* 2 large fresh tomatoes, skinned
> 1 cup tomato juice or water
> ½ t. salt

[4 SERVINGS]

HEAT oil. Brown meat well on all sides, a few pieces at a time. Return meat to pan and sprinkle with 1 teaspoon salt, pepper, and cinnamon. Add 1 cup water, cover pan, and simmer for 1 hour or longer, until lamb is tender.

While meat cooks, peel eggplant and cut lengthwise in 6 to 8 wedges. Salt lightly and drain pieces in colander for 30 minutes.

Meanwhile, soak rice in water to cover for 30 minutes.

Pat eggplant dry. Fry in hot oil until golden to dark brown on all sides. Drain on absorbent towels placed over newspaper.

Brown whole garlic in same oil for a minute or two. Place eggplant and garlic over tender meat and cover with drained stewed tomatoes or a layer of thickly sliced tomatoes. Cover pan and simmer 10 minutes. Add tomato juice or water and bring to boil. Drain rice. Add with ½ teaspoon salt to meat. Push rice gently down into juices with back of spoon.

Reduce heat, cover pan, and simmer 20 to 25 minutes longer, until rice absorbs all the liquid. Turn off heat. Set pan aside for 10 minutes to fluff rice.

Serve hot with yoghurt spooned over the top.

• LAMB STEW WITH CIDER VINEGAR • OR LEMON JUICE

LAHUM-T-KHAL

Either cider vinegar or lemon juice is added at the end of the cooking time to obtain the stew's unusual tartness. Each, of course, has a separate and distinctive flavor. I believe vinegar originated as an alternative to lemon juice when lemons were scarce and expensive here in the States.

> 3 – 4 T. vegetable oil
> 1 pound lamb shoulder or beef, cut into stew chunks
>
> · · ·
>
> 1 – 2 cups coarsely chopped onions
> ¾ cup water
>
> · · ·
>
> 1 t. salt
> ⅛ t. freshly ground pepper
> 2 cups water
>
> · · ·
>
> 6 small whole peeled onions, 1½ inches in diameter
>
> · · ·
>
> 4 T. flour
> 4 T. cold water
> ⅓ cup cider vinegar or fresh lemon juice

[4 SERVINGS]

HEAT oil and brown meat on all sides, frying a few pieces at a time. Remove from pan with slotted spoon and set aside. In same fat, sauté onions until translucent and medium-dark brown around the edges. Add ¼ cup water and stir to begin dissolving onion. When water is absorbed, add

¼ cup more water and cook until water is absorbed again. Repeat a third time. Onion will be a mushy and fragmented purée.

Return meat to skillet. Add salt, pepper, and 2 cups water. Cover pan and simmer a total of 1½ hours, until meat is very tender. Thirty to 45 minutes after simmering starts, add small whole onions. The meat and onions should become tender simultaneously.

Mix together flour and 4 tablespoons water to make a smooth paste. Add cider vinegar or lemon juice. Stir this paste into bubbling sauce and cook 10 minutes, until gravy thickens.

Serve hot over rice.

• GROUND-MEAT-WITH-PINE-NUT- • FILLING "STEWS"

YAKHNIT LAHUM MAFROUM

These recipes are quick to put together. Use *coarsely* ground lamb if you can get it. A basic cooked meat filling, which is also one of the *kibbeh* stuffings, is simply topped with spinach or layered with tomatoes and baked. For other *kibbeh* stuffings, see index.

If you intend this as your main entrée, double the amount of stuffing.

I. WITH SPINACH: *YAKHNIT SABANEKH*

1 recipe basic cooked meat stuffing, with onion (see page 158)

• • •

**1 pound fresh spinach, leaves and stems, *or* 2 ten-ounce packages
    frozen spinach, thawed**
1 lemon

[4 SERVINGS]

PREPARE basic stuffing in a skillet or suitable covered pan you can bring to the table.

Wash spinach. Do not shake dry. Place spinach on top of meat filling in pan and cover tightly. Cook over moderate heat until spinach is tender, 10 to 15 minutes. (If using thawed spinach, arrange over stuffing; cover and simmer 5 to 8 minutes.)

Uncover and cook 5 minutes longer to evaporate juices and thicken sauce. Squeeze juice from half a lemon over "stew" and cut remaining half into wedges.

Serve directly from the pan onto a bed of rice. Good with yoghurt spooned over the top.

II. WITH TOMATO

1 recipe basic cooked meat stuffing (see page 158)

· · ·

6 large ripe tomatoes
Salt and freshly ground pepper

[4 SERVINGS]

SPOON stuffing between thick layers of sliced tomatoes; cover and bake at 350° for 1 hour. Uncover during last 30 minutes to reduce juices a bit. Salt and pepper to taste.

Serve hot over rice.

III. WITH GREEN BEANS, TOMATOES, AND ONION

This version takes longer to bake, for you are actually substituting a ground meat stuffing for the lamb chunk layer in green bean oven stew. For a more vegetable-oriented casserole with some meaty flavor, use one recipe of cooked meat stuffing instead of two.

2 recipes basic cooked meat stuffing (see page 158)

· · ·

3 large onions, sliced thick
6 large fresh tomatoes, sliced thick, _or_ 1 quart stewed tomatoes

· · ·

1 pound fresh green beans
Salt and freshly ground pepper

[6 SERVINGS]

SPREAD basic meat stuffing on the bottom of a 3½- to 4-quart casserole. Cover with a thick layer of onions. Place half the tomatoes over the onion. Lay washed and trimmed beans over this, and top with remaining tomatoes. Salt and pepper to taste.

Cover casserole and bake a total of 1½ hours at 325°. Uncover during last 30 minutes to reduce juices.

Serve with rice. Good with yoghurt on the side and Arabic bread.

· XIV ·

FATTEES

*F*ATTEES are layered dishes based on dried bread which has been toasted golden brown in butter. Meats or chick peas, rice, pine nuts, and a garlic-yoghurt sauce transform stale bread, a potential "throw-away," into a delicious experience. *Fattees* are wonderful to serve to a group of friends, not only because they are beautiful (mounds of white-mantled eggplant, chicken, or tongue bespeckled with green parsley and brown pine nuts), but because their nature demands they be eaten in entirety. We *have* eaten leftover *fattee*, but you really miss the crunchy bread texture which makes this dish so special. The bottom layer of toasted bread absorbs juice from the meat or chick peas and sponges up the creamy yoghurt. Do not delay between assembly and table!

The nature of the dish is such that you can expand or contract amounts quite easily to serve however many you want to, even one or two. It's easy to visualize the infinite possibilities of variations on this theme of bread and garlic yoghurt.

• CHICKEN *FATTEE* •

FATTEE DJAAJ

Stages of this elegant and delicious dish can be prepared ahead of time, so you can enjoy your company! Aunt Alice's version has a few whole cloves plus ¼ teaspoon ground cloves added to the rice as it cooks. She omits the vinegar-garlic sauce, adding garlic to the yoghurt instead, and uses this yoghurt as the first liquid layer over the bread. Her next layer is rice with more yoghurt smothering the plate. Around the white pyramid, a necklace of chicken pieces and bread triangles. Pine nuts, parsley, and paprika decorate the whole. Lovely! Lovely! Lovely!

Cousin Leila suggests adding 1 – 2 tablespoons *tahini* to each 2 cups yoghurt for a subtle variation in flavor. Try this with any of the *fattee* recipes.

A 4–5 pound stewing or roasting chicken
1 quart water
1 t. salt
1–2 sticks cinnamon

· · ·

3 loaves Arabic bread: 2 dried, 1 fresh (or 3 fresh)
6 T. melted butter

· · ·

¼ cup pine nuts
2 T. butter or oil

· · ·

1 cup chicken broth (from above)
3 cloves garlic, crushed
1 T. red wine vinegar

· · ·

1 t. salt
1 cup raw long-grain rice
2 cups chicken broth (from above)

· · ·

3–4 cups thick yoghurt, at room temperature
½ t. salt

· · ·

3 T. finely chopped parsley

[6 OR MORE SERVINGS]

WIPE off chicken and put in pot with 1 quart water, 1 teaspoon salt, and cinnamon sticks. Bring to boil. Reduce heat, cover, and simmer 1 hour, until tender. Remove meat from bones and break into large chunks. Strain broth. Reserve 3 cups. Place meat in ovenproof dish and cover with enough broth to moisten it well. Set aside.

Toast breads according to directions on page 20 and set them aside. Brown pine nuts carefully in 2 tablespoons butter or oil and drain them on paper towel to remove excess fat. Put them in a bowl for later use.

Thirty minutes before serving, reduce 1 cup chicken broth by a quarter and stir in garlic and vinegar; keep this warm. Heat chicken in 300° oven.

Add 1 teaspoon salt and rice to 2 cups reserved chicken broth, bring to a boil, then reduce heat and simmer for 20 minutes, until liquid is absorbed. Cover rice and let it sit a few minutes until ready to assemble *fattee*. Season yoghurt with ½ teaspoon salt.

Just before you are ready to sit down, do the final assembly. Place broken toasted breads on large platter. Pour reduced and flavored broth over them. Spread a bed of rice on the bread and arrange chicken over this. Cover with yoghurt. Decorate with chopped parsley and pine nuts. A sprinkle of paprika adds color. Arrange toasted triangles of bread around platter and enjoy.

· CHICK PEA *FATTEE* ·

FATTEE BI HUMMOUS

Spearmint may be sprinkled over final layer or mixed into all layers of yoghurt for this *fattee*.

¾ **cup dry chick peas, soaked overnight**

· · ·

3 loaves Arabic bread: 2 dried, 1 fresh (or 3 fresh)
6 T. melted butter

· · ·

¼ **cup pine nuts**
2 T. butter or oil

· · ·

3 – 4 cups thick yoghurt, at room temperature
½ **t. salt**
1 large clove garlic, crushed
2 T. crushed dried spearmint

[3 TO 4 SERVINGS]

COOK chick peas until very tender, about 1¼ hours. Drain, reserving ½ cup juice. Prepare bread (see directions for crisping bread on page 20). Brown pine nuts carefully in butter or oil and set aside. Season yoghurt with salt, garlic, and spearmint (or reserve spearmint for top layer only).

Layer half of the bread in the bottom of a deep dish and moisten with some of the reserved chick pea juice. Cover with half the chick peas and half the yoghurt. Repeat layers of bread, chick peas, and yoghurt. Sprinkle pine nuts (and spearmint, if saved) over the top and serve immediately.

• EGGPLANT *FATTEE* I •

FATTEE BATINJANN I

Aunt Celia introduced us to this *fattee* on paper. Aunt Alice gave us *fattee mak-doos*, a variation distinguished by the tart, strange, and mysterious flavor of pomegranate syrup.

10 – 12 cylindrical eggplants (about 2 pounds), 4 – 6 inches long

· · ·

½ cup pine nuts
3 T. butter

· · ·

1 pound ground lamb
1 t. ground cinnamon
1 t. salt
¼ t. pepper

· · ·

4 T. vegetable oil

· · ·

2 – 3 cups tomato juice
Salt and freshly ground pepper as needed
Pinch sugar

· · ·

3 loaves Arabic bread: 2 dried, 1 fresh (or 3 fresh)
6 T. melted butter

· · ·

3 cups yoghurt
1 large clove garlic, crushed
½ t. salt

· · ·

2 T. finely chopped parsley

[6 TO 8 SERVINGS]

WASH eggplants but do not peel. Cut off stems. Using reamer, hollow out eggplants very carefully, leaving shell ⅛ to ¼ inch around. Save the pulp to make eggplant dip – see page 75.

Fry pine nuts in 3 tablespoons butter over low heat until evenly browned all over. Brown lamb until it loses red color and sprinkle in cinnamon, 1 teaspoon salt, and ¼ teaspoon pepper. Stir all but 2 tablespoons pine nuts into mixture.

Spoon or push meat filling into eggplants, firmly but not too compactly. You want the filling to stay in as you fry the eggplants. Brown stuffed eggplants in oil for a few minutes, turning several times.

Place stuffed eggplants in pan to fit (try a 3-quart size) and cover with tomato juice flavored with salt, pepper, and a bit of sugar. If you have a loose fit, place an inverted plate on top of eggplants to weight them down. (Juice should cover plate.)

Bring to boil, reduce heat, and simmer, partially covered, for 30 to 45 minutes, until eggplants are tender. You don't want to overcook them and get mush or all the work will have been for naught.

While eggplants are cooking, crisp bread as directed on page 20. Stir garlic and salt into yoghurt and bring to room temperature.

When eggplants are tender, arrange bread on a large platter and sprinkle with ½ cup tomato juice. Pattern eggplants on top of bread and mask with yoghurt. Sprinkle with reserved pine nuts and chopped parsley; paprika, too, for color. Serve immediately.

• VARIATION •
FATTEE MAKDOOS

Use the recipe above, but with a couple of distinctive changes. Chop 1 medium onion and fry with meat. Add cinnamon, 1 teaspoon salt, and ¼ teaspoon pepper. When mixture has cooled a bit, stir in 1 tablespoon chopped parsley. Add 1 tablespoon pomegranate syrup (see page 7) to each cup tomato juice used. Salt and pepper to taste. For layering up, it's bread, juice, yoghurt, and the eggplants arranged on top, then sprinkled with pine nuts and parsley.

• EGGPLANT *FATTEE* II •
FATTEE BATINJANN II

Tahia Alamadeen, a friend of the family, once surprised us with this *fattee*. She prepared it full of lamb chunks and succulent wedges of large round eggplant, covered with the incomparable goat yoghurt so readily available in Lebanon.

1 pound lamb bones
1 pound lamb, cut into chunks
1 quart water
1 t. salt
1 stick cinnamon

. . .

2 large round eggplants (2¼ pounds)
1 cup vegetable oil

. . .

2 cups broth (from above)
Salt to taste
¼ t. freshly ground pepper
⅛ t. ground allspice

. . .

¼ cup pine nuts
2 T. butter

. . .

Bread, yoghurt, and parsley as for the preceding *fattee* (see page 238)

[6 SERVINGS]

COVER bones and meat with 4 cups water in a large pan. Bring to boil, skimming froth. Add salt and cinnamon stick.

Reduce heat, cover, and simmer 1¼ to 1½ hours, until meat is very tender. Strain off broth. Remove bones and stick cinnamon from meat. If necessary, reduce broth; you'll need 2 cups. Return meat and broth to large pan. Add pepper and allspice. Taste and add salt if needed. This may be set aside and heated just before serving.

While meat is cooking, peel eggplants and halve lengthwise. Cut each half into 4 or 5 long wedges. Salt lightly and drain wedges in colander for 30 minutes. Brown pine nuts in butter over low heat. Drain on paper toweling and set aside. (To increase the absorbency of disposable toweling, place a thick layer of newspaper under a double layer of paper towels.) Prepare bread, yoghurt, and parsley.

Pat eggplants dry. Fry until medium-dark brown in hot oil. Drain on rack or paper.

Ten minutes before you are ready to eat, reheat meat and simmer uncovered for 5 minutes. Then place fried eggplant over meat and simmer 5 minutes to heat eggplant and blend flavors.

To assemble, arrange toasted bread on platter and spoon over enough juice to moisten bread well. Arrange lamb and eggplant and cover with yoghurt. Decorate with pine nuts, parsley, and paprika. Place triangles of bread around the edges.

• TONGUE *FATTEE* •

FATTEE BI LISANAT

(from Aunt Helen)

Tongue is a delicate, soft-textured meat, often neglected or shied away from for reasons such as the one Walter frequently used as a small child. Question: "How do you know you don't like it?" Response: "It *looks* like I don't like it." Nevertheless, we've received more than polite acceptance of this dish even from those friends who aren't particularly fond of this cut. For those of you who don't have reservations and actually enjoy tongue, this is a wonderful recipe.

1 beef tongue *or* 6 – 7 lamb tongues
3 – 4 cups water
1½ t. salt
5 – 6 peppercorns
1 bay leaf
1 onion, slivered in thin crescents
1 potato, peeled and quartered
1 carrot, peeled and sliced

· · ·

1 cup dry chick peas, soaked overnight

· · ·

3 loaves Arabic bread: 2 dried, 1 fresh (or 3 fresh)
6 T. melted butter

· · ·

¼ cup pine nuts
2 T. butter

· · ·

3 – 4 cups thick yoghurt, at room temperature
1 large clove garlic, crushed
½ t. salt

· · ·

2 T. finely chopped parsley

[6 TO 8 SERVINGS]

SIMMER tongue with water, seasonings, onion, potato, and carrot for 2 to 2½ hours, until tender; or pressure cook 45 minutes and let pressure drop of its own accord. Split and skin soaked chick peas as directed on page 73. Cook them in soaking water until tender, about 20 minutes. Crisp bread (see page 20), using 6 tablespoons butter. Brown pine nuts carefully in 2 tablespoons butter and set aside. Stir garlic and ½ teaspoon salt into yoghurt, using larger amount for luxury.

When tongue is done, remove and cool enough to handle, reserving broth. Skin and cut into ¼-inch slices, or cut into chunks. Strain some broth over meat and place in ovenproof dish. Twenty minutes before serving, heat tongue and chick peas separately in 300° oven. When they are hot, assemble *fattee*. Over toasted broken bread pieces, spoon several tablespoons broth and a layer of warm chick peas. Arrange tongue over this and cover with yoghurt. Decorate with pine nuts and parsley, and arrange bread triangles around platter.

DESSERTS

FRIED BREAD
Zalaybee
246

SPOON DOUGHNUTS IN SYRUP I
Awwammat I
247

SPOON DOUGHNUTS IN SYRUP II
Awwammat II
248

RICE PUDDING WITH TOP MILK
Roz bi haleeb
249

SHORT-CUT RICE PUDDING
Muhalabieh
251

SPICED RICE PUDDING
Mughlee
252

NUT-FILLED FLAKY PASTRY
Baklawa
253

SEMOLINA AND YOGHURT CAKE
Nammura
254

SAFFRON SHORTBREAD
Sfoof
255

BUTTER COOKIES
Ghoraybee
256

WALNUT- OR DATE-FILLED SEMOLINA COOKIES
Maamoul
257

DATE CONFECTION
Tamer bi jawsd
259

Ordinarily, the arrival of a bowl of fresh fruit announces the end to a Lebanese meal: succulent figs, the juicy prickly pear cactus fruit, tree-ripened pears, peaches, and apricots. The climate is well suited to nurturing a wide variety of fruit, as we discovered while visiting Uncle Salim in Baakline during the month of August.

He took great pride in walking us through his lush green orchard, which lay terraced on the arid rocky mountainside. Olive groves and hanging arbors of grapes complemented the rows of mulberry, pear, peach, lemon, orange, fig, and apricot trees, to name a few. Salim insisted we try a fruit from every tree, to see how exquisite the dead-ripe fruit could be. I did so with obedience and pleasure. At the end of an hour, however, I was wondering how Walter could still have an appetite, when I noticed he was taking only one bite of each fruit, rather than consuming the entire thing. The measure of restraint and wisdom!

Dried fruit, such as figs and apricots, are also commonly served for dessert along with nuts—especially pistachios and almonds. *Amareddeen*, a popular sweet similar to what we call "fruit leather" in the United States, is made from perfectly ripe apricots pressed into a thick, deep-orange-colored sheet. Small pieces or strips of this confection satisfy after-dinner cravings. And on occasion a rice pudding flavored with orange flower water might be served.

When special dinners demand exotic delicacies (nut-filled, many-layered, rich, flaky pastries flavored with rose or orange flower water and saturated with honey or syrup), a short journey to the local bakery is in order. An abundance of excellent bakeries rules out the need to make the majority of rich pastry desserts, cookies, or confections at home. That is, until you find yourself back in the New Country, without such access. We experienced some difficulty locating home recipes for traditional dessert specialties such as *ghoraybee*, the rich butter cookie, the traditional *baklawa*, or the lovely mold-formed nut- or date-filled semolina cookie, *maamoul*. Walter's aunts pulled through, however, and brought some recipes to light. These have been tested with much weight-gain as a result!

Included here is only a sample, a small tasting of the sweet side to Old Country cookery. Visit your local Arabic bakery for the full range of sweet pleasures.

• FRIED BREAD •

ZALAYBEE

Zalaybee are wonderful for breakfast, either fried or baked. Mix the dough up the night before and let the yeast work while you sleep.

> 1 T. (1 package) dry yeast (see page 20)
> ½ cup warm (110°) water
> 1 t. sugar
>
> · · ·
>
> 1 cup milk, scalded
>
> · · ·
>
> 1½ – 2 t. salt
> 4 cups unbleached white flour
>
> · · ·
>
> Vegetable oil for frying

[ABOUT 2 DOZEN]

PROOF yeast in water with sugar for 5 minutes. Cool scalded milk to 110°. Add to yeast and mix well. Sift salt and flour together. Quickly stir milk mixture into flour, working well. You may wish to finish mixing the dough with your hands, dipped in oil. Then on a lightly floured board knead dough well, until elastic, about 5 minutes. Place in greased bowl, cover with cloth, and set aside until doubled – or refrigerate and let slow-rise overnight.

Punch dough down. (If refrigerated, let come to room temperature for about 1 hour.) Knead for a minute or two, then tear off pieces of dough about the size of an egg; flatten them into oblongs that are 2 inches wide by 6 to 7 inches long and ¼ inch thick. Stretch them between your palms. Poke 2 or 3 holes in each oblong.

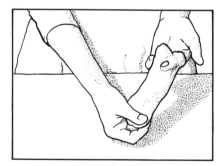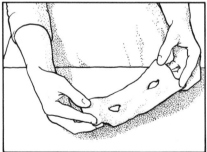

Heat ½ inch oil in skillet to 375° and fry bread pieces until they are golden brown on both sides. Drain on paper towels laid over newspapers.

Serve hot with butter and honey; or dip them while hot into cool orange flower water syrup (see page 247); or sprinkle with granulated sugar.

· VARIATION ·

If you're worried about calories, form dough as above, but do not fry. Let rise until doubled (1 hour). Bake at 375° for 10 to 12 minutes, and serve as above.

· SPOON DOUGHNUTS IN SYRUP I ·

AWWAMMAT I

Awwammat are literally dough nuts, small nut-sized pieces of dough deep fried, then soaked in simple syrup, which may or may not be flavored with orange flower water. They are dense, sweet, and rich, and greatly loved by children of all ages. One recipe includes yoghurt; the other includes both potato and yeast.

ORANGE FLOWER WATER SYRUP

4 cups sugar
2 cups water
2 T. orange flower water (see page 6)
2 t. fresh lemon juice

DOUGHNUTS

3 cups flour
¼ t. baking soda
½ t. salt

. . .

1½ t. pure vanilla extract
2 cups yoghurt

. . .

Vegetable oil and olive oil *or* lard for frying

[70 TO 80 BALLS]

BRING sugar and water to low boil. Reduce heat and simmer 15 minutes. Off heat, stir in orange flower water and lemon juice. Set aside to cool by setting pan in cold water.

Then prepare doughnuts. Sift flour, baking soda, and salt together. Stir vanilla into yoghurt and add to flour mixture. Mix well until dough holds together and turn out onto floured board. Knead a minute or two. Cut into 5 or 6 strips and flour well for easier handling.

To form and fry *awwammat*, pour oil into heavy deep pot and heat to 375°. Take dough in left hand (if you are right-handed) and make hazelnut-sized chunks by cutting them off with spoon held in right hand. One strip of dough makes a good batch, but stop before adding the whole strip if you notice the oil temperature dropping much below 375°. When balls are golden brown around the edges, turn them over and fry other side. Remove with slotted spoon. (Be *sure* to remove all doughnuts from each batch or you may find an exploding overdone ball in your lap.) Drain only a second on paper toweling and quickly plunge into cold syrup. Let them soak a few minutes until the next batch is ready to be removed from the hot oil. Remove finished doughnuts to serving dish.

• SPOON DOUGHNUTS IN SYRUP II •

AWWAMMAT II

The orange rind makes the difference in this version of *awwammat*. Yeast provides a lighter, looser dough. To insure crispness of outer skin of *awwammat*, keep pan of syrup in a bowl of ice as you dip the finished doughnuts. Syrup tends to warm with repeated dunkings of hot *awwammat* and you want to avoid this.

1 recipe orange flower water syrup (see page 247)

. . .

1 – 2 potatoes, to yield 1 cup mashed

. . .

1 T. (1 package) dry yeast (see page 20)
1 t. sugar
1 cup warm (110°) water

. . .

2 T. rose flower water (see page 6)
Rind of 1 orange, grated

. . .

2½ cups bread or unbleached white flour
1 t. salt
Vegetable oil or lard for frying

[40 OR MORE LARGE DOUGHNUTS; 70 TO 80 SMALL DOUGHNUTS]

CHILL syrup until you begin to fry dough. Peel, slice, and boil potatoes until soft. Mash well. Measure out 1 cup.

Dissolve yeast and sugar in water. After 5 minutes, whisk yeast mixture into potato. Beat in rose water and orange rind.

Stir flour and salt together. Add all at once to potato mixture and thoroughly combine. Work dough well with wooden spoon; mixture will be sticky but cohesive. Cover bowl and let rise until double, about 1 hour. Stir dough down. Sprinkle a little flour over dough and stir lightly with rubber scraper so dough pulls away from side of bowl. If dough seems too sticky to handle (it was for us), add a bit more flour and work it with spoon into dough.

Oil hands. Follow *awwammat I* instructions (on page 247) for forming, frying, and syrup dipping. Or make even free-er form doughnuts, cutting dough off a larger spoon with a smaller spoon or knife.

• RICE PUDDING WITH TOP MILK •

ROZ BI HALEEB

Rich top milk, or cream, can be poured over the cooked rice pudding, which is then baked in the oven, gaining a wonderful brown crust of gold! Aunt Celia is a master of this one. The secret to success with this version is to use short-grain starchy rice.

1 cup raw short-grain rice
1½ cups water
1 t. salt

   . . .

2 quarts whole milk

   . . .

⅔ – 1 cup sugar
2 T. orange flower water (see page 6)

   . . .

½ cup or more heavy top milk, cream, or evaporated milk (optional)

[10 TO 12 SERVINGS]

PLACE rice in bowl and wash under cold running water until water runs clear. Bring 1½ cups water to boil in a heavy 4-quart pan and stir in salt and rice. Reduce heat, cover pan, and simmer 20 minutes, until water is absorbed.

Scald milk and stir into rice; be sure to scrape the bottom of the pan to dislodge any stuck rice. Cook over moderate heat until very thick and creamy, about 45 minutes, stirring frequently with a wooden spoon so milk does not scorch. Mixture will reduce some. Pudding ought to look like thick lumpy white sauce.

Add sugar and stir a few minutes. Then continue to cook over moderate heat an additional 10 to 15 minutes, until it is again very thick. Continue to scrape and stir often.

Add orange flower water and blend well. You should have about 8 cups of rice pudding.

You may omit the remainder of the recipe and instead just pour finished pudding into individual serving dishes to cool. If you do this, apricot preserves or canned apricot halves with syrup can be spooned over. However, since the beauty of the dish is the cream layer, it is worth the extra effort.

First choose appropriate baking dishes: Walter suggested using two small dishes instead of one large pan, in case you weren't planning to serve the pudding all at once. That way you could keep half with the crust intact for another occasion. A 2½- to 3-quart casserole or 9½-by-13-by-2-inch baking pan works fine for 12 people. Otherwise two 8-inch square pans will do. Pudding is traditionally poured 2½ to 3 inches deep, but about 2 inches also works well.

Pour pudding into baking dishes. Gently pour enough top milk, cream, or evaporated milk over the top until it just covers, forming a thin layer. Bake uncovered at 350° until a brown wrinkly crust of gold forms (30 to 40 minutes). Serve warm or at room temperature.

Recipe may be halved. If so, reduce initial cooking time from 45 minutes to 30 minutes. After sugar is added, cook additional 5 to 7 minutes. Bake as usual for 30 to 40 minutes with rich cream layer.

· SHORT-CUT RICE PUDDING ·

MUHALABIEH

This is a quicker, finer-textured version of rice pudding that has served us well for years. The assembled pudding looks remarkably like a perfectly cooked fried egg. Needless to add that all further resemblance ends there. Sitti did not use salt in this recipe.

> **5 cups milk**
> **½ t. salt**
> **1 cup cream of rice (see Note)**
>
> · · ·
>
> **½ cup sugar**
> **2 T. orange flower water (see page 6)**
>
> · · ·
>
> **2 cups canned apricot halves**
>
> [6 TO 8 SERVINGS]

SCALD milk and stir in salt. Sprinkle cereal over milk and cook on low heat, stirring constantly, for 10 minutes. It will be very thick. Remove from heat and stir in sugar. Continue stirring 2 minutes. Then add orange flower water and blend well. Spoon into individual serving dishes and cool.

Place an apricot half on each serving and cover with several tablespoons apricot syrup.

NOTE: You can make your own cream of rice. Pulverize 1 cup raw short-grain rice in blender until texture resembles coarse cornmeal. Cooking time will be 15 minutes, instead of 10 minutes. Add sugar and cook 5 to 10 minutes longer, then continue recipe as above.

• SPICED RICE PUDDING •

MUGHLEE

A very sweet pudding, traditionally served when a male child is born. Apparently the *mughlee* pudding is served to visitors paying their respects to a mother of a new son. A newborn daughter's visitors get plain *mughlee* tea. Time will hopefully let girls into the pudding league as well. From Libby: "This is one of the best recipes that I know of for *mughlee*. Good luck...P.S. Serve cold with blanched almonds and walnuts which have been soaked in water and peeled; also with shredded coconut, pine nuts, and pistachios."

> ½ cup water
> 1 piece dried gingerroot, the size of an unshelled almond
>
> • • •
>
> 6½ cups water
> 1¾ cups sugar
> 1 t. ground cinnamon
> 1 t. caraway
> 1 t. ground anise
> ½ t. ground cloves
> 1 cup pulverized raw rice
>
> • • •
>
> Pine nuts, blanched almonds, soaked walnuts, pistachios,
>   and shredded coconut
>
> [12 SERVINGS]

In a covered pan, boil gingerroot in ½ cup water for 30 minutes. Remove ginger. In a large saucepan, add more water if necessary to gingerroot tea to equal ½ cup. Grind spices together in a blender to form a powdery mixture or, if you prefer, crush the spices using a mortar and pestle. Mix rice, sugar, and spices together with tea and 6½ cups water. Cook over medium heat, stirring until it comes to a boil. Reduce heat and continue cooking slowly for about ¾ hour, stirring frequently. Pudding should be thick and creamy.

Pour into dessert dishes while hot. Chill. Decorate with nuts and shredded coconut.

All babies deserve equal treatment.

• NUT-FILLED FLAKY PASTRY •

BAKLAWA

One of the decadently delicious heavy, rich after-dinner sweets purveyed and popular in the Middle East. The Druse influence has made its impact on the Norwegian waistline in Mount Horeb, Wisconsin, due to the popularity of homemade *baklawa* at school bake sales!

1 pound walnuts or pistachios, or a combination, chopped
2 t. ground cinnamon
½ cup sugar
    • • •
½ pound butter, melted
1 pound filo dough (see page 6)
    • • •
2 cups honey
1 cup water
1 T. fresh lemon juice
1 cup sugar
    • • •
2 T. rose or orange flower water (see page 6)

[60 PIECES]

COMBINE nuts with cinnamon and ½ cup sugar. Brush baking pan (9 by 13½ inches or larger) with some melted butter. Taking one sheet of filo, start at the top of one side of pan. Bring sheet across bottom and run it up other side. Brush with butter. Fold in any "overhang" to use as start for second sheet. Begin second whole sheet of filo where first left off and complete second layer. Brush with butter. Fold over sheet to make third layer.

Repeat brushing and layering until you have 12 layers of filo. Sprinkle one third of nut mixture on twelfth layer; cover with another 2 layers of filo. Brush with butter. Sprinkle another third of nut mixture and cover with 2 buttered sheets. Repeat one more time. Layer and brush remaining filo sheets. Mark in diamond pattern, using a very sharp knife or a single-edge razor blade, penetrating 2 or 3 layers of filo. Bake at 300° for 1½ hours. Check during last 20 minutes. If it is not browning golden enough to suit your taste, raise temperature to 325° for remainder of cooking time.

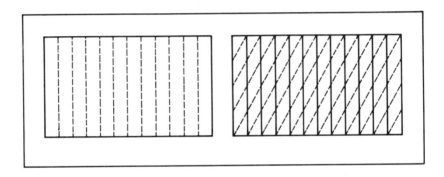

While it bakes, bring honey, 1 cup water, lemon juice, and sugar to a boil. Reduce heat and slow-boil for 5 minutes, watching carefully. Stir in rose or orange flower water. Cool by placing pan in cold water. It is very important to pour cold syrup over hot *baklawa*, so you may even want to chill the syrup. (Hot syrup over hot *baklawa* turns into a soggy mess.) Pour cold syrup over hot *baklawa* as soon as it emerges from the oven.

• SEMOLINA AND YOGHURT CAKE •

NAMMURA

This is delicate in flavor, heavy in texture. A small sweet bite of *nammura* with rich dark coffee makes your meal or midday pause complete.

2 cups semolina (see page 7)
4 T. butter

. . .

½ t. baking soda
1 t. baking powder
½ t. salt
1 cup sugar

. . .

2 cups yoghurt

. . .

2 cups sugar
⅛ t. salt
1 cup water

. . .

2 T. orange flower water (see page 6)

[20 PIECES]

HEAT semolina and butter together over low heat. Work butter into semolina until it is completely melted and absorbed. Add baking soda, baking powder, ½ teaspoon salt, and 1 cup sugar. Blend well. Stir and shake pan so semolina does not burn.

Pour in yoghurt. Take pan off heat and stir well to combine completely. Pour into an 8-inch square pan or equivalent, and let batter rest for 2 hours.

While batter rests, make a syrup: dissolve 2 cups sugar and ⅛ teaspoon salt in 1 cup water over low heat. Bring to boil and simmer 15 to 20 minutes. Stir in orange flower water. Cool by placing pan in cold water, then chill.

Bake *nammura* at 375° for 45 to 55 minutes, until crust is lightly browned on top and slightly hard like a thin shell. It may show signs of slight cracking. When cake is done, score it into 20 diamonds or squares, then cut all the way to the bottom of the pan. Pour *cold* syrup over *hot* cake. Syrup will all be absorbed.

This dessert ages well.

• SAFFRON SHORTBREAD •

SFOOF

Saffron is traditional for this shortbread as it is neither as scarce nor as dear in Lebanon as it is in the States — for good reason: accessibility. On one of her forays into the Lebanese hills, Aunt Libby gathered great fluffy orange-red bags of it. There may be a dearth of birds in Lebanon, but saffron, no!

Sue Hamady provided us with the following *sfoof* recipe, which calls for turmeric ("poor man's saffron") — an acceptable substitute, though the flavor is not as subtle as saffron.

1¼ cups (2½ sticks) butter, melted

. . .

4 cups flour
2 cups sugar
2 t. baking powder
1 t. saffron or turmeric
½ t. salt

. . .

⅔ cup milk

. . .

1 – 2 T. milk
1 – 2 T. pine nuts

[40 PIECES]

M ELT butter. Cool to lukewarm by placing pan in cold water. Sift flour with sugar, baking powder, saffron or turmeric, and salt. Stir butter into flour mixture until flour is well moistened. Rub mixture together between palms, "smearing" the butter and flour until all lumps are gone. Mixture will resemble coarse cornmeal. This may take a few minutes, but it thoroughly works the butter into the flour mixture. Poke several holes in mixture and pour ⅔ cup milk into holes. Stir with fork only enough to incorporate liquid so dough holds together.

Grease a 9-by-13-inch baking dish and pat dough evenly over the bottom, pressing down firmly. Brush with a few tablespoons of milk. Decorate with pine nuts placed at 1½- to 2-inch intervals. Bake at 350° for 30 to 35 minutes, until crust becomes light brown and a toothpick inserted in the middle pulls out clean.

Cool. Cut into 40 squares with a pine nut in each center.

• BUTTER COOKIES •

GHORAYBEE

A rich shortbread cookie, from a recipe sent via Aunt Libby. A bit of salt brings out the flavor, but it's not traditional.

8 T. or 4 ounces butter
¾ cup confectioners sugar

. . .

2 cups unbleached white flour
¼ t. salt

. . .

Pistachios, pine nuts, or slivered blanched almonds

[20 TO 24 THREE-INCH RING COOKIES]

CREAM butter until very light and fluffy. Sift sugar and gradually beat into butter until creamy again.

Sift flour with salt. Stir flour into butter mixture until all is well combined. Divide dough in 4 or 5 balls.

To form cookies, roll each ball into a ½-inch rope. Cut each into lengths about 6 inches long, and form into rings. Space cookies at least an inch apart on cookie sheet. Decorate rings with a few pistachios, pine nuts, or slivered blanched almonds.

You may also form dough into rounds, ⅓ to ½ inch thick, and decorate each round with a whole blanched almond in the center.

Bake at 300° for 20 minutes, until barely colored on the bottom. Be careful not to brown them. Cool 10 minutes before removing from cookie sheets.

· WALNUT- OR DATE-FILLED · SEMOLINA COOKIES

MAAMOUL

These are traditional Easter cookies. Aunt Alice has given me her off-the-top-of-her-head instructions, which I compared to other *maamoul* recipes found Stateside. She stressed the old pie dough technique: rub in shortening well; then sprinkle water over the mixture and toss it lightly together. Avoid overworking the dough. *All* the other recipes advised kneading the dough well. So there you have it. Alice's *maamoul* are memorable. Do not expect the dough to be cohesive, but it will be damp enough to form into balls to pack into the cookie molds (see page 4).

This recipe needs to be started a day ahead.

½ cup solid shortening
8 T. or 4 ounces butter

. . .

1 cup flour
2 cups semolina (see page 7)
¼ t. salt
¼ t. baking powder
¼ cup granulated sugar

. . .

2 T. rose flower water (see page 6)
1 T. orange flower water (see page 6)
7 T. water

. . .

One of the fillings (see below) or some of each
Confectioners sugar

[25 MAAMOUL]

MELT shortening and butter together, or use all butter if you wish a richer cookie. Cool slightly. Mix flour, semolina, salt, baking powder, and sugar together. Rub melted shortening into dough with fingertips until it is like fine soft meal. Cover bowl and let it rest overnight.

Combine flower waters with 7 tablespoons water and sprinkle over the dough. Toss lightly with a fork to distribute liquid evenly. Mix until just combined, like pie dough.

Dust *maamoul* molds well with flour. Invert and tap gently to remove excess flour.

Estimate amount of dough needed to fill *maamoul* mold and make a ball of dough. Flatten it out slightly and place a good tablespoon of filling in center. Close dough around filling to cover it. Pack ball into mold. Level off cookie even with the lip of the mold; be sure you haven't revealed filling, or it will stick to the pan as it bakes.

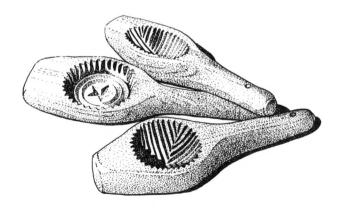

Tap cookies out onto the work area with a sharp firm hit to the top of the mold. Transfer cookies to baking sheet with a spatula. Bake at 300° to 325° about 12 minutes, until barely colored. Cool. Sprinkle or rub with confectioners sugar before serving.

WALNUT (OR PISTACHIO) FILLING

1¼ cups finely chopped walnuts or pistachios
2 T. orange flower water
¼ cup sugar
¼ t. ground cinnamon

Mix all together well.

DATE FILLING

Date filling is traditionally used with a flat *maamoul* mold, rather than the mounded variety.

1½ cups chopped dates
6 T. butter

Cook dates with butter over low heat for 15 to 20 minutes. Mash occasionally until dates are completely puréed. Cool before filling.

• DATE CONFECTION •

TAMER BI JAWSD

One sweet bite...We were told to "mash dates with butter and cook until mushy. Pound walnuts until soft and mix into dates and butter. Roll in balls. Roll in coconut." If these proportions are traditional, it's purely coincidence, but we *did* gain them through experience.

6 T. butter
1½ cups (12 ounces) firmly packed chopped dates
. . .
1½ cups (6 ounces) crushed walnuts
. . .
½ cup (2 ounces) shredded coconut

[30 TO 35 BALLS]

Melt butter over low heat. Add dates and mash together with butter. Cover pan and cook for 15 minutes, mashing and stirring frequently. They ought to be soft enough by then to smash with a spoon into a smooth paste. While they cook, crush walnuts with mortar and pestle. Stir nuts into smooth date paste and mix well. Consistency should be fairly solid.

Roll into small balls and roll them in coconut.

· XVI ·

BEVERAGES

SPICED TEA WITH PINE NUTS, ALMONDS,
AND WALNUTS
Mughlee tea
264

ARABIC COFFEE
Qahweh
265

ORANGE BLOSSOM "COFFEE"
Qahweh baida
265

ABOUT THE GLASS OR THE CUP

T H E Lebanese do not drink much wine with their meals, if any. For some, religion bars the addition of alcohol to the table; for others, tradition recommends water or a licorice-flavored liquor called *arak* which is frequently mixed with water. *Arak* turns the water into a cloudy brew that is sipped along with either the *maza* or the main meal. Dry white wine is a suitable accompaniment for Lebanese cooking. Serve it chilled or with unorthodox ice cubes.

Two traditional drinks are *mughlee* (refreshing aromatic anise-ginger tea sweetened with honey, in which blanched almonds, walnuts, and pine nuts floated and sank, popping up again like so many submarines in a cup) and *qahweh* (strong thick Arabic coffee served in a demitasse and sweetened according to occasion or taste). Lebanese coffee is, strictly speaking, Turkish coffee. Arabic coffee as the Gulf Arabs prepare it is quite different and requires a special mode of preparation. Often the coffee is more heavily laced with sugar when served alone than when served with a dessert. Ground cardamom seed may be added to the cup, along with a few drops of flower water, another option. When properly made, the coffee has a light foam on top. If the host or hostess is thoughtful, a bit of foam will be poured into each visitor's cup, for the foam is a sign of good fortune.

• SPICED TEA WITH PINE NUTS, •
ALMONDS, AND WALNUTS

MUGHLEE TEA

This fragrant tea is traditionally given to friends visiting a newborn female child; the male child rates the *mughlee* pudding. It is wonderful any time at all and is extremely refreshing and delicious. Asian food stores carry dried gingerroot.

> 2 quarts water
> 2 pieces dried gingerroot, 1 inch long
> 2 sticks cinnamon
> 1½ t. whole cloves
> ⅓ cup anise seeds, sorted and rinsed
>
> • • •
>
> ½ cup walnut halves
> ½ cup pine nuts
> ¼ cup whole almonds

[8 SERVINGS]

BOIL water with spices in a covered enamel or stainless steel pan for about 1 hour. Strain tea.

Meanwhile blanch walnuts, pine nuts, and almonds in separate dishes of boiling water for 2 minutes to remove any bitterness. Rub skins off almonds and split them. Drain nuts and place them in separate serving dishes.

Serve tea, allowing guests to add three varieties of nuts. Sweeten to taste with honey.

• ARABIC COFFEE •

QAHWEH

For every demitasse (⅓ cup) water use:

> ½ – 1 t. sugar
> 1 heaping t. Arabic coffee (preferably freshly roasted and ground
>   extremely fine or pulverized)
> Ground cardamom
> Orange flower water (see page 6) (optional)

M EASURE water as needed into Arabic coffeepot. Stir in sugar and bring to boil. Stir once again to be sure sugar is dissolved. With pot off heat, stir in coffee. Return to heat and bring to boil over high heat.

When foam reaches top of pot, take it off the heat and let foam fall, or tap pot gently against the side of the stove. I have seen people give the pot a good hard bang, so don't be too precious about it.

Return coffee to heat and bring to boil again. Repeat tapping and heat a third time, but do not tap pot this time around; sprinkle a few drops of water over coffee to make the foam fall. (Aunt Hajar told us to "reserve" a demitasse of boiling water and after the third rising of the foam, to add it to the pot and cover with a plate for a minute. This helps to settle the grounds.)

Pour immediately into serving cups, making sure everyone has some foam, for this is regarded as good luck. Sometimes ground cardamom seed is added to the pot or individual cup, and/or a drop of orange flower water.

• ORANGE BLOSSOM "COFFEE" •

QAHWEH BAIDA

This recipe arrived in a letter from Leila. "There is also a drink referred to as 'café blanc' or *qahweh baida*, white coffee, which is actually clear.

"Boil water and add 1 to 2 drops of orange flower water to a cup, with or without sugar – real light and digesting." (love, Leila)

· GLOSSARY ·

ARABIC : English

AAJEEN : dough

ADASS : lentils

ALLAH : God

AMAREDDEEN : dried pressed apricot paste

ARDISHAWKI : artichoke

BABA GHANNOUJ : eggplant purée with *tahini*, lemon, and garlic

BAKDOUNIS : parsley

BAKLAWA : nut- and honey-filled filo dough, a Middle Eastern pastry

BAKLEE : purslane

BAMIEH : okra

BANADOURA : tomato

BASSALL : onion

BATINJANN : eggplant

BATTATTA : potato

BAYD : egg

BHAR : black pepper

BURGHUL : partially cooked cracked wheat, usually available in 3 sizes

CAM-MOON : cumin

DEHEN : lamb fat base, with small bits of cooked lamb and spices (also called *qawarhma*)

DIBS RIMMAN : pomegranate syrup

DJAAJ : chicken

FARAYKEE : wheat roasted when green, smoky in flavor

FATAYER : pies, turnovers

FATTEE : bread-based entrée : layers of bread, yoghurt, rice, with meat, vegetables, chick peas, etc.

FATTOUSH : salad using dried Arabic bread as base

FETA : commonly known as *jibneh Bilgharieh*, or Bulgarian cheese: a salty white sheep milk cheese

FILO : paper-thin sheets of pastry, used mainly for desserts such as *baklawa*

FOOL : fava beans

GHORAYBEE : ring-shaped butter cookies

HALEEB : milk

HAMOD : lemon

HAREESEE : wheat soup

HUMMOUS : chick peas; often meaning the chick pea – *tahini* dip

IJJEE : omelet/fritter

JAWSD : walnuts

JIDDI : grandfather

KEFTA : ground meat with parsley, onion, and spices

KERFEH : cinnamon

KHAL : vinegar

KHUBUZ : bread

KHUDRA : vegetables

KHYAR : cucumber

KIBBEH : ground meat, *burghul*, onion, and spices; a national dish of Lebanon

KISHIK : yoghurt, wheat, and milk fermented, dried, and ground into a floury substance

KIZBARA : coriander

KOOSA : green cylindrical summer squash, covered with a fuzz somewhat like peach skin; closest American equivalent is zucchini

LABAN : yoghurt: cultured milk

LABNEE : drained yoghurt with consistency of cream cheese

LAHUM : meat; usually refers to lamb

LAKHTEEN : pumpkin

LIFT : turnip

LISANAT : tongues

LOUBIEH : green beans

MAAMOUL : molded semolina cookies filled with nuts or dates

MAHSHI : anything that is stuffed

MAKBOOS : pickled

MAKHLUTA : mixed dried bean soup

MAKLEE : fried

MALFOOF : cabbage

MARAQAH : marinade type sauce

MAWARD : rose blossom water

MAZA : hors d'oeuvre: a tradition in itself

MAZAHER : orange blossom water

MENAZZALEH : fried eggplant with tomato, chick peas, and onion

MILEH : salt

MISHWEE : broiled, cooked, baked

MUGHLEE : refers to a spiced rice pudding or a tea served when a child is born

MUJADDARAH : lentils with rice and onion

NAA-NAA : spearmint

QAHWEH : coffee

QARNABEET : cauliflower

QAWARHMA : see *dehen*

ROZ : rice

SABANEKH : spinach

SĀJJ : steel dome used as baking surface for mountain bread

SALATA : salad

SAMAK : fish

SAMBOUSEK : hot pastry filled with meat or cheese

SANEEYEH : oven pan

SFEEHA : meat pies (also called *lahum bi aajeen*)

SHAMANDAR : beets

SHEESH BARAK : pastries stuffed with meat or other filling, cooked in yoghurt or sumac sauce

SHISH KEBAB : meat and vegetables cooked on a skewer

SHOURABA : soup

SILQ : Swiss chard

SITTI : grandmother

SMEED : semolina: ground "hearts" (endosperm) of hard wheat

SNOBER : pine nuts

SOUM SOUM : sesame

SUMMAK : sumac: purple berries with a tart flavor

TABBOULEH : classic tomato, spearmint, parsley, wheat (*burghul*) salad; not to be confused with hot *tabbouleh*

TAHINI : sesame seed paste made from cold ground toasted sesame seeds

TARATOOR : sauce of *tahini*, lemon, salt, and garlic

TOOM : garlic

WARAK AREESH : stuffed grapeleaves (also known as *warak inab*)

YAKHNIT : stew

YENSOON : anise

ZAATAR : Arabic for thyme, often meaning mixture of thyme, sesame seeds, and ground sumac

ZA'FARAN : saffron

ZALAYBEE : fried bread, sugared or dipped in syrup

ZEIT : oil

ZEITOON : olives

CONVERSION TABLES

All the recipes in this book are based on American nonmetric measure. On the following pages are some conversion charts and other useful measures giving nearest convenient equivalents.

AMERICAN LIQUID (Nonmetric)	IMPERIAL LIQUID

1 U.S. ounce = 1 Br. ounce

3 teaspoons (t.) = 1 tablespoon (T.)	3 teaspoons = 1 tablespoon (T.)
2 T. = 1 ounce	2 T. = 1 ounce
16 T. = 1 cup = 8 ounces	20 T. = 1 cup = 10 ounces
2 cups = 1 pint = 16 ounces	2 cups = 1 pint = 20 ounces
2 pints = 1 quart = 32 ounces	2 pints = 1 quart = 40 ounces
4 quarts = 1 gallon = 128 ounces	4 quarts = 1 gallon = 160 ounces

METRIC

Liquid

1 U.S. teaspoon = 5 millilitres (ml)
1 U.S. tablespoon = 15 ml
1 U.S. cup = ¼ litre (L)
1 U.S. pint = ½ L
1 U.S. quart = 1 L
1 U.S. gallon = 4¼ L

Dry

1 U.S. pint = ½ litre (L)
1 U.S. quart = 1 L

SOLID MEASURES

American/British	Convenient metric equivalent
1 U.S. ounce	30 grams (g)
1 U.S. pound = 16 ounces	450 g
2.2 U.S. pounds	1000 G = 1 kilogram (k)
3½ ounces	100 g

LINEAR MEASURES

⅜ inch = 1 centimetre (cm)
1 inch = 2½ cm

OVEN TEMPERATURES

Fahrenheit	Centigrade	Descriptive term
Up to 225°	Up to 110°	cool
225° – 275°	110° – 135°	very slow
275° – 325°	135° – 165°	slow
325° – 400°	165° – 205°	moderate
400° – 450°	205° – 230°	hot
450° – 500°	230° – 260°	very hot
500° and up	260° and up	extremely hot

USEFUL EQUIVALENTS

VEGETABLES

1 large cauliflower = 1½ – 2 pounds
1 large eggplant = 1 pound
3 large onions = 1 pound
1 large onion, chopped = 1 cup
3 – 4 medium potatoes = 1 pound
4 – 5 medium tomatoes = 1 pound
5 – 6 small zucchini = 1 pound

GRAIN AND BEANS

flour: 3½ cups = 1 pound
rice and wheat: 2½ cups dry = 1 pound
       1 cup dry = 2 – 2½ cups cooked
chick peas: 3 cups dry = 1 pound
       1 cup dry = 2½ – 3 cups cooked
lentils: 2½ cups dry = 1 pound = 5 cups cooked

NUTS AND SEEDS

pine nuts: 4 cups = 1 pound
tahini (sesame paste): 2 cups = 1 pound
walnuts: 4 cups = 1 pound

MISCELLANEOUS

dry milk: 4 cups nonfat = 1 pound
       = 1 gallon rehydrated
eggs: 4 – 6 large = 1 cup
honey: 2 cups = 1 pound
oil: 2¼ cups = 1 pound
sugar: 2½ cups = 1 pound
yeast: 1 T. dry = ⅔-ounce compressed cake